THE ROCKEFELLER REPORT ON THE AMERICAS

THE ROCKEFELLER REPORT ON THE AMERICAS

The Official Report of a
United States Presidential Mission
for the Western Hemisphere,
by Nelson A. Rockefeller

THE NEW YORK TIMES EDITION

With an Introduction by Tad Szulc of
The New York Times

Chicago
QUADRANGLE BOOKS
1969

 For information, address the publisher at 12 East Delaware Place, Chicago 60611. Manufactured in the United States of America. Published simultaneously in Canada by Burns and MacEachern Ltd., Toronto.

Library of Congress Catalog Card Number: 78-108447

INTRODUCTION

by Tad Szulc

Latin America has been analyzed, studied, dissected, researched, surveyed, and X-rayed by the United States in the last quarter of a century as no other region of the world. It has been the object—if not always the ultimate beneficiary—of American policies and political philosophies spanning a period of nearly 150 years and ranging from James Monroe's Doctrine to Teddy Roosevelt's Manifest Destiny, from Franklin D. Roosevelt's Good Neighbor era to John F. Kennedy's Alliance for Progress.

But all these studies, doctrines, policies, and programs seem to have eluded the objective of building a viable and constructive relationship between the United States and the southern part of the hemisphere. Depending on the mood and the emergencies of the moment, Latin America has been variously regarded in Washington as our "safe backyard" and the fertile ground for American political and economic expansion, or as our "soft underbelly," first menaced by the Nazis and the Japanese in World War II and currently by the Soviet Union and the native but dangerously exportable communism of Premier Fidel Castro.

With this fluctuating relationship, Latin Americans have developed toward the United States a love-hate syndrome. They have tried to adopt our democratic and constitutional pattern and to model themselves after the great American success story while at the same time resenting us for what we are and how we have acted. The Yankees, for their part, have lived through a curious succession of indifference, guilt-ridden bursts of action toward the hemisphere, and, finally, fear of what may happen there.

It has been, then, an uneven, ill-balanced, and frustrating

relationship for both sides, despite rhetorical assurances of good will and understanding flowing at appropriate times from Washington as well as most of the Latin American capitals.

Castro's advent to power in Cuba in 1959 was a milestone in the sense that not only the Cubans but many other Latin Americans, including friends of the United States, began to address the "Colossus of the North" with increasingly and brutally frank talk about what was wrong between us. To be sure, concern over Latin America, the awareness of the problems, and the deteriorating relations did not await Castro's appearance on the scene. In 1953 and 1958, President Eisenhower dispatched his brother, Dr. Milton S. Eisenhower, to survey Latin America and recommend new policies to him. Richard M. Nixon, as Vice-President, had a violent introduction to the hemisphere's problems in the spring of 1958 during his tour of the region.

The first steps toward correcting our lopsided relations with Latin America followed these visits and reports, but the United States took no spectacular action until the Kennedy administration launched in 1961 its Alliance for Progress, raising to an unprecedented level Latin American hopes and expectations for a better life.

Many Americans seemed to think that with the Alliance and its aid and reform programs all was well again in our "backyard." Castro was contained on his Caribbean island; preoccupied with new and grave problems at home and abroad, Americans once more turned away from Latin America, presumably satisfied that the winds of revolution, nationalism, and anti-Yankeeism had died down, at least in this generation.

This, however, is not the case, and the documented proof that the situation in Latin America is worse and more dangerous at the close of the 1960's than it was at the beginning of the decade is provided in the report written for President Nixon by Governor Rockefeller and his advisers after visiting twenty hemisphere nations in the spring and summer of 1969.

Governor Rockefeller is not an alarmist by nature, and his exposure to Latin America in public life goes back to the wartime days of the early 1940's when he served as FDR's coordinator for Inter-American Affairs. I have no idea—and I am sure that the Governor himself would not recall it offhand—how many times he has been to Latin America, how many countries there he has visited in the last twenty-five years, and with how many thousands of Latin Americans he has talked during all these years as a government official, special envoy, or businessman with extensive interests in several hemisphere nations. Suffice to say that Mr. Rockefeller's Latin American experience in depth is matched by few Americans, and, accordingly, his words must carry weight and should command attention.

These words in his report to President Nixon are an attempt to warn Americans that the hemisphere is again in the throes of violent political, economic, and social convulsions which, he tells us, threaten "more Castros" in Latin America. Put another way, the Governor is saying that concerned as we are with the war in Vietnam, with the Middle East, with the problems of race and urban ghettos and universities and the whole galloping social revolution at home, we would do well to take a new and fresh look at Latin America before it is too late.

Past administrations as well as critics of our Latin American policy have long been warning that it may soon "be too late" in the hemisphere, and various policies have been tailored to deal with this whole disturbing relationship.

Under the Alliance for Progress programs, both the Kennedy and Johnson administrations tried to find solutions through accelerated aid to Latin America and through an insistence on internal reforms—in land tenure, tax structures, and so forth—that would render U.S. assistance really meaningful. But, as events have demonstrated, American aid was not always wisely given or used, despite the huge amounts involved, and the Latin Americans themselves have fallen considerably short of keeping their end of the bargain on self-help and basic reforms. In Washington, bureaucratic red tape and a maze of legislative obstacles and impediments frequently turned the aid programs into inefficient or unfeasible undertakings. The men in power in Latin America just as frequently chose to ignore their commitments to reform for domestic political considerations and the other reasons. In the end, then, the results have been disappointing and, instead of gaining sympathy, the U.S. found itself deeply resented in the hemisphere.

To compound matters, the Latin American birthrate has far outstripped these assistance and development efforts—thus causing social tensions even more powerful than those of a decade ago—and new political forces have come to the fore with a new sense of nationalism and anti-American sentiment. Governor Rockefeller makes a sound and realistic judgment that unless all these trends are reversed, the U.S. may well find itself isolated in the hemisphere in the 1970's.

Mr. Rockefeller implies at the same time that an American isolationism—stemming from a general weariness with world problems, or expressed through trade protectionism practiced under the law, or as a policy influenced by what he calls "special-interest" groups—would inevitably quicken the process of isolating the U.S. from its "backyard." Quite aside from whether new Castros would or would not emerge in Latin America—and the Governor thinks they well may—such an isolation would pose catastrophic economic and foreign policy problems for this country.

The Governor's analysis of the "quality of life in the Americas" is highly perceptive in observing that the forces that traditionally supported the old status quo in Latin America—the Roman Catholic Church and the military—are now turning toward progressive attitudes. On the surface, the U.S. should welcome this as a positive phenomenon. But in practice this new state of affairs is creating tough dilemmas for the U.S., and Mr. Rockefeller is not blind to them.

The Church, as he has recognized, now increasingly favors reforms. But, as recent pronouncements by Latin American churchmen have shown, the young clergy, the "worker priests," and politically active leftist Catholics are blaming the U.S. for much that is wrong with life in Latin America. A section of the Church is, then, becoming an additional channel for intensive nationalism and, axiomatically, for anti-Americanism.

The military, once a pillar of conservatism, not to say of reaction, are moving into the forefront of nationalistic forces, and they too are speaking with anti-American overtones. On the one hand, the U.S. cannot but approve of their reformist zeal. But, on the other hand, the fact that several of the military regimes have won power by overthrowing democratic governments is disturbing to Americans. When they nationalize U.S. property—as Peru and Bolivia have done in the last year or so—Washington tends to develop mixed feelings about the military reformers. And, finally, these regimes are ideologically unpredictable, as the Governor has noted, and may go in any doctrinal direction. This may mean a form of authoritarian socialism known in the Middle East as "Nasserism," or just plain rejection of U.S. presence and influence.

In the old days, U.S. policy was to do no business, or as little business as possible, with Latin American dictators. Dr. Eisenhower had recommended this kind of aloofness as long ago as 1953 when he drafted the first report on Latin America for his brother, the President. President Kennedy broke relations with military dictatorships that ousted democratic regimes and deprived them of economic aid. This was an ideological position that, looming as a simple black-and-white situation, made sense to a great many Americans.

But the nature of Latin American dictatorships has changed, and this is a fact the U.S. must take into consideration, disagreeable as it might be to those dedicated to the cause of Latin American diplomacy. Inasmuch as five out of ten South American republics are now ruled by military regimes—some of them more and others less reform-minded—there seems to be little choice for the U.S. but to live with them at the risk of deepening the process of isolation. Governor Rockefeller has proposed the pragmatic concept that diplomatic relations should not constitute moral approval, and that our dislike of a regime must not deprive the people of that country of the economic aid they need. This is a proposition that certainly merits serious thought and, as Sir Harold Nicolson once remarked, foreign policy must not be based on enthusiasm or sentiment.

Having thus recognized many of the Latin American realities and the frustrations and tensions that accompany them, Governor Rockefeller has come up with an astonishingly outspoken series of specific recommendations as to how we can best live with Latin America and how best she can be aided in the midst of her awesome economic problems.

The Governor is a Republican, but he has served Democratic administrations and his report on Latin America is free of partisanship. He admits that the Kennedy-initiated Alliance for Progress raised expectations that could not be met, but he recognizes that through the Alliance valuable lessons were learned that can now serve as the basis for new policies.

In the minds of many of the young leftist Latin Americans who rioted against him during his fact-finding trips, Mr. Rockefeller may be associated with vested U.S. economic interests. His name alone evokes memories of an economic past in Latin America that he and many other Americans would prefer to forget at the threshold of the 1970's. But Governor Rockefeller's recommendations—many of them now espoused by President Nixon as U.S. policy—are strikingly imaginative and far-reaching. Possibly to the surprise of his Latin American detractors—and possibly shocking to American businessmen—he speaks out against "special-interest" groups in the U.S. whose influence has had an adverse effect on the quality and efficiency of American aid.

In proposing preferential trade treatment for Latin America and other underdeveloped countries, the Governor has set in motion what may be a new revolution in world trade and a source of unhappiness for many U.S. "special-interest" groups. But, endorsed by President Nixon, his ideas are a major breakthrough in trade policies with repercussions to be felt not only in Latin America but throughout the "Third World."

The report offers other specific recommendations on how the U.S. can best assist Latin America to cope with her heritage of centuries of economic and social imbalance. It stresses the need for refinancing the huge Latin American foreign debt—debt repayments in some cases now exceed the new aid inflow—and it emphasizes development of education, health, and housing. It proposes to do away with much of the Washington-based bureaucracy, never a popular move in this capital. And, not unimportantly, it insists on the resumption of personal relationships between Americans of the North and the South.

Quite evidently, reports such as Governor Rockefeller's cannot by themselves change a situation fraught with tensions and dangers. But no policy can be evolved without a conceptual basis, and in providing his perceptive and flexible analysis and recommendations Mr. Rockefeller has gone unexpectedly far in establishing foundations for policies that must not be Nixon policies but United States policies.

CONTENTS

Introduction by Tad Szulc v

Letter to the President 5

List of Advisers 11

Foreword 15

Preamble 17

Chapter One: Quality of Life in the Western Hemisphere 21

A. The Special Relationship in the Western Hemisphere 21

B. The Existing Situation 22

C. Forces of Change 24

Communications 25
Science and Technology 25
Population Growth 27
Urban Life 27
Nationalism 29
Young People 30
Labor 30
The Cross and the Sword 31
The Church 31
The Military 32
Business 33
Communist Subversion 34
Changes in the Decade Ahead 35

Chapter Two: The Challenge to Political and Economic Freedom 37

A. The Nature of the Challenge 37

B. The United States' National Interest 38

C. Our National Objective 39

Chapter Three: Organization 43
A. Organization of United States Government 43
1. Create Secretary of Western Hemisphere Affairs 45
2. Create Western Hemisphere Policy Director and Staff 46
3. Create Economic and Social Development Agency 46
4. Create Institute of Western Hemisphere Affairs 47
5. Support Overseas Private Investment Corporation 48
6. Create Joint Congressional Committee 49
B. Country-by-Country Relations 49
C. Regional Organizations 51
1. Provide Financial and Technical Assistance 52
2. Appoint Assistant Secretaries to CACM, LAFTA, and CARIFTA Nations 52
3. Air Transport Facilities for Assistant Secretary 52
D. Inter-American Organizations 52
1. Political Recommendations 53
2. Economic and Social Recommendations 53
3. Education, Science, and Cultural Recommendations 54
4. Security Recommendations 54
5. CECLA 54
E. International Organizations 55
1. Bi-lateral and Regional Assistance Programs 55
2. Avoid Isolationism 55

Chapter Four: Policy and Action 57
A. United States Political Relations with the Hemisphere 57
B. Western Hemisphere Security 59
C. Economic and Social Development 65
1. Trade Policies 70
Tariff Preferences 75
Aid United States Workers 76
Readjust Import Quotas 76

Fair Prices 77
Coffee 77
Sugar 80
Regional Markets 80
Shipping Conferences 80
2. Development Assistance 80
AID Impediments 81
Program Loans 85
Project Loans 86
Western Hemisphere Development Committee (OAS) 86
Low-Interest Rates 86
Repeal Additionality 86
Broaden Restrictions 86
Modify Present Policy on Assistance Cutoffs 87
Repeal Shipping Restriction 87
3. Debt Service Problems 87
Generous Rescheduling 88
Survey (CIAP) 88
Using Local Currency Funds 88
4. Private Savings and Investment 88
Tax Rules 89
Contract Mechanism 93
OPIC 93
Smaller Companies Combining 94
Developing Entrepreneurs 94
Local Savings, Open-End Investment Trusts .. 94
Uniform Rules 95
5. Urban Development and Housing 96
Rehabilitate United States Cities 100
Total Community Development 100
Better Loan Programs 100
Joint Efforts 101
Promote Individual Participation 101
D. The Division of Labor 101
Hemisphere Conference 103
E. Education, Science, and Culture 104
$100 Million Financing of Institute 115
Powers of Institute 115
F. Labor 116
Labor Representation in Developmental Planning 117

American Institute for Free
Labor Development 117

G. Agriculture 117
Reform Development and Agrarian
Reform 124
Opening United States Markets 124
Demonstration Programs 124

H. Conservation 125
Inter-American Institute of
Natural Resource Conservation 127
Classify Problems 128
Information Program 128
Training Program 128
Public Works Program 128

I. Health 128
Infant Mortality 129
Water 129
Hunger 131
Birth Control 131
1. Nutrition Program 135
2. Support Multilateral Groups 135
3. Tropical Medicine 136

J. Women 136

K. Communications 137
Stepped-Up Program 139
Match Radio Havana 139
Special Team to Visit Media in United States . . 139
Greater Exchange 139

Chapter Five: Conclusion 141
People 141
Western Hemisphere as a Unity 141
Crossroads 142
Interdependence of the Hemisphere 143
The United States as an Example 143
A Course of Action 143
Major Policy Statement 144

THE ROCKEFELLER REPORT ON THE AMERICAS

"Forces are now converging that make possible, for the first time, the hope that many of man's deepest aspirations can at last be realized . . .

"We seek an open world—open to ideas, open to the exchange of goods and people, a world in which no people, great or small, will live in angry isolation."

President Richard M. Nixon
Inaugural Address
January 20, 1969

The Honorable Richard M. Nixon
The White House
Washington, D.C.

Dear Mr. President:

I enclose the final report and recommendations based on the findings of the mission you requested me to undertake. If I may, I should like to take this opportunity to review briefly the developments from the time of your original call.

It was on your first full day in the White House that you asked me to undertake the mission, to consult with the leaders of the other American republics on your behalf, and to help your administration develop policies for the conduct of our international relations throughout the Western Hemisphere.

Your decision to set up such a mission was bold, sensitive, and significant. Here was the newly inaugurated leader of the most powerful nation in the world, at the very outset of his administration, seeking the advice and counsel of the leaders of our neighbor states before formulating his policies as they related to Western Hemisphere affairs. This development, in my opinion, has given promise of a new era of consultation and close cooperation in international relations.

Only through consultation in the development of common objectives is it possible for the nation-states today to work out common policies and joint programs that will truly represent the best interests of all. In thus initiating this program of extensive consultation at the highest levels, you were embarking on a new approach at a crucial point in Western Hemisphere relations.

As I am sure you will recall, Mr. President, you first discussed this mission with the distinguished Secretary General of the Organization of American States, Señor Galo Plaza, whom you received on your first day in the White House—and it was his suggestion that I be asked to head the mission.

I immediately felt, when you called me, that it was an exciting and unique idea. As I said at the time, however, your request presented me with a difficult problem. On the one hand, I have long had an abiding faith in and affection for our neighbors in the hemisphere—and a deep belief in the importance of Western Hemisphere unity to our mutual security and well-being.

On the other hand, as Governor of New York State, I had a great responsibility to meet a growing fiscal crisis and the urgent human needs which exist in our state as they do throughout the nation. These had to be dealt with first. The New York State Legislature was in session and my obligations to the people of New York State naturally had priority.

You were very understanding of this dilemma, and you made it possible for us to work together toward finding solutions to the critical needs of the states. You gave me the opportunity to make a full presentation at the White House on these matters to you and the Urban Affairs Council and to put before you the Governors' recommendations for new federal policies. Your expressed concern at that meeting was a beginning of the change of federal-state relationships which you have so significantly been carrying forward. This together with your early decision to seek substantially increased federal aid to state and local governments, with reforms in welfare and other fields, was a vital assurance to me and to the other Governors that help was on the way. A key to the future solution of the acute fiscal problems of the states and localities was about to be turned.

Finally, there was your understanding acceptance of the fact that our trips throughout the hemisphere could not begin until the New York State Legislature had adjourned, and would have to be broken into four journeys with time in between to maintain direction of the affairs of the State.

In preparing for the mission, it was obvious that the basic facts concerning the problems and aspirations of the nations of the Western Hemisphere were well known. It was equally obvious, however, that we in the United States had not found effective answers as to how we should solve the problems and more effectively cooperate in meeting the aspirations on a basis of mutual interest.

In view of the wide range of the areas of common concern

among the peoples of the Western Hemisphere, and because there were twenty-three countries to visit, each with its own special problems, it seemed clear to me that I could not do this job alone. It would have been impossible for one person to spend enough time in each country to talk with all the key people in the various areas in both public and private life. Therefore, I invited a group of outstanding citizens of the United States to go with me. Each was an expert in a specialized field—such as trade, finance, education, science, culture, women's activities, agriculture, labor, and other fields. The names of these citizens who gave so generously and so effectively of their time and talents on these missions appear at the end of this letter.

Twenty to twenty-five of these distinguished advisers were on each trip. In each country, a schedule of visits with the key people was worked out in advance of our arrival. While I was meeting with the President or Prime Minister of the country, and later with the Minister of Foreign Affairs and often with the entire cabinet, each of the advisers would be meeting with leaders, both public and private, in fields of common interest and concern. In this way, the advisers on your mission were able to visit and counsel with some one hundred to two hundred people in each country. It would have taken weeks in each country for one person to cover the same ground in similar depth. Furthermore, no one could have the combined expertise of the advisory members of your mission. They are an extraordinary group of men and women, and they served their country selflessly and brilliantly. Through this letter, I would like to share with you my profound admiration and deep gratitude for the contribution they have made.

Through these saturation visits, the members of your mission were able to sit down and talk, as knowledgeable colleagues, with experts of all sorts on specific problems and to gain new and sensitive insights on what could be done more effectively to achieve our common objectives. I must also take advantage of this letter to say to you, Mr. President, how grateful and appreciative we are for the time and invaluable advice these outstandingly able leaders from public and private life in the various countries gave to the members of your mission.

Each member of the mission has written detailed reports on his findings, all of which will be part of the final record. In addition, intensive group discussions were held during and after our travels. This group effort and the invaluable counsel it produced are reflected in the findings of this report. However, no attempt was made to achieve a consensus, and I accept sole responsibility for the recommendations in the report.

In addition to being able to communicate directly with national leaders, I was also able to communicate with the people of each country through press, radio, and television interviews.

We not only listened to the problems, hopes, and aspirations of the people and the leaders of the other American republics, but also were able to get their advice and counsel and their assessment of the political realities of today. Deeper understanding and new approaches to solutions of our common problems resulted.

As everyone knows, the mission encountered difficulties. The new military government of Peru stated that our visit would be "inconvenient" and requested indefinite postponement. This action was the result of a specific incident, growing out of the dispute between the United States and Peru over fishing rights and expropriation of oil fields, but it was unrelated to our mission.

After a student was accidentally shot and killed in a demonstration during the mission's early visit to Honduras, student groups, stimulated by subversive elements on an organized basis throughout the hemisphere, used the incident as a rallying point in attempting to prevent our visits or to disrupt them. As a result of these demonstrations and the threats of violence, together with certain delicate internal political situations, the governments of Chile and Venezuela also asked us to postpone our visit, thus reducing to twenty the number of countries on our itinerary.

Suggestions have been made that the trips were ill timed and should have been canceled. In actual fact, the trips were very well timed; they were timed to the opportunity and will of a new administration to formulate a new policy for the hemisphere. And it became clear as our trips progressed that without such a new policy the nations of this hemisphere would steadily and rapidly become less disposed—because of disillusionment and cynicism—to deal candidly and effectively with the United States and with confidence in the mutuality of our interest and good will.

In any case, the timing had nothing to do with the demonstrations and violence that occurred; they can be attributed to these causes: There is general frustration over the failure to achieve a more rapid improvement in standards of living. The United States, because of its identification with the failure of the Alliance for Progress to live up to expectations, is blamed. People in the countries concerned also used our visit as an opportunity to demonstrate their frustrations with the failure of their own governments to meet their needs. In addition, demonstrations that began over grievances were taken over and exacerbated by anti-U.S. and subversive elements which sought to weaken and discredit the United States, and their own governments in the process. It is significant that these same elements were active in demonstrations, threats, and acts of violence in democratic countries as well as in those with military governments. In fact, one mission member remarked that the only frightening confrontation of all our travels was that caused by an SDS-organized student demonstration at John F. Kennedy International Airport as we returned to New York City at the end of our fourth trip.

Had we canceled the visits, it would have been seen as weakness and fear on the part of the United States government. This would have done much to discredit the United States in the other Americas. It would, moreover, have undermined the priority and importance which you attach to the hemisphere's needs. Thus it would have lost us as a nation an opportunity —one that is increasingly rare—to work out our common problems for our common benefit. As it was, by carrying out the mission despite the difficulties, the determination and purposefulness of the new administration were clearly evidenced. The reception that the mission received from government officials and from leaders in private fields was open and warm.

One important by-product of the demonstrations and violence was that they put the mutuality of the problems of our hemisphere on the front pages of our newspapers, on the nation's television screens, and therefore in the minds of most Americans. It is unfortunate that these problems only get attention in this fashion. If we in the mission served as a lightning rod—if we focused attention on the deep-rooted nature of the hemisphere's concerns and what should be done about them—the difficulties and criticism that we encountered were well worth it.

I appreciated the opportunity of keeping in touch with you during our trips and visiting with you between trips, for in this way I was able to give you a general review of our findings as we went along. And I am delighted that some specific actions have already been taken as a result. You have already received the reports on my personal conversations and observations in each country.

This report is based on the mission's findings, checked against many other sources. One that was particularly helpful was the constructive report of the House Subcommittee on Inter-American Affairs, headed by Representative Dante Fascell. We also acknowledge the cooperation of the respective chairmen of the Senate Foreign Relations Committee and the House Foreign Affairs Committee. I would particularly like to express my gratitude for the interest, cooperation, and participation of the State Department.

May this report, with its recommendations, help you to serve the cause of better relations and progress for all people in the Western Hemisphere.

With warm best wishes,

Respectfully,

NELSON A. ROCKEFELLER

New York, New York
August 30, 1969

ADVISORY MEMBERS OF THE MISSION

George Beebe, Senior Managing Editor, *Miami Herald*

Victor Borella, Special Assistant to the Governor of New York for Labor Affairs

David Bronheim, Director, Center for Inter-American Relations

Dr. Detlev W. Bronk, Past President of the National Academy of Science, Johns Hopkins University and the Rockefeller University

William F. Butler, Vice-President and Chief Economist of the Chase Manhattan Bank

James M. Cannon, Special Assistant to the Governor of New York

Miss Evelyn Cunningham, Director, Women's Unit, State of New York

Dr. Gordon F. Ekholm, Curator of Mexican Archaeology, American Museum of Natural History

Dr. Robert Goldwater, Chairman, Administrative Committee, Museum of Primitive Art, and Professor of Fine Arts, New York University

Dr. Harold B. Gotaas, Dean, Technological Institute, Northwestern University

Dr. Samuel B. Gould, Chancellor, State University of New York

Dr. Walter D. Harris, Jr., Associate Professor of City Planning, Department of Architecture, Yale University

John B. Hightower, Executive Director, New York State Council on the Arts

Mrs. Patricia Hitt, Assistant Secretary of Health, Education and Welfare

Dr. G. Kenneth Holland, President, Institute of International Education

Thomas P. F. Hoving, Director, Metropolitan Museum of Art

Frederic K. Howard, Consultant, Inter-American Development Bank

Mrs. Flora Kampmann, former Republican National Committeewoman for Texas

Augustine R. Marusi, Chairman and President, Borden, Inc.

Mrs. Dorothy McHugh, Republican National Committeewoman for New York

Andrew McLellan, Inter-American Representative, AFL-CIO

Dr. Alan D. Miller, Commissioner of Mental Hygiene, State of New York

Dr. Emil M. Mrak, Chancellor Emeritus, University of California at Davis

James Noel, Jr., Director for Central America and the Caribbean, Catholic Relief Services, U.S. Catholic Conference

Gen. Robert W. Porter, Jr., USA (Ret.), former Commander-in-Chief, U.S. Southern Command

Dr. Clark W. Reynolds, Associate Professor of Economics, Stanford University

Dr. W. Kenneth Riland, Chief Physician, New York, U.S. Steel Corporation

Col. John D. Silvera, Program Coordinator, New York State Office on Urban Affairs

Samuel P. Singletary, Special Assistant to the Governor of New York

Rev. Wyatt Tee Walker, Special Assistant to the Governor of New York for Urban Affairs

Arthur K. Watson, Chairman of the Board, IBM World Trade Corporation, former President of the International Chamber of Commerce

Dr. Leroy Wehrle, Fellow, Institute of Politics, Harvard University

Dr. Clifton R. Wharton, Jr., Vice-President, Agricultural Development Council

Monroe Wheeler, Counsellor to the Trustees, Museum of Modern Art

Thomas H. Wolf, Vice-President and Director of Television Documentaries, ABC News

George D. Woods, Consultant, First Boston Corporation and former President, World Bank

Special Advisers
Richard Aldrich
John R. Camp
Jerry Danzig
Col. John Deaver
Berent Friele
John W. Johnston, Jr.
Jerome I. Levinson
Kenneth M. Rabin
Dr. Hyman Zuckerman

Advance Group
Joseph H. Boyd, Jr., Director
Ronald Abney
Joseph W. Canzeri
Henry Diamond
David Duffy
Theodore Halaby
Kenneth T. Hoeck, Jr.
Lincoln Hoffman
George Humphreys
James Kiepper
A. Bruce Manley
John W. McGrath
John Moss
Joseph E. Persico
David Reif
Craig Thorn III
Jerald I. Wolfgang

Staff
Elizabeth Boyd
Ann Boylan
Flor Brennan
Harold Brown
Rodney Campbell
Arline Cherniak
Ann Coleman
Evelyn Cook
William Eckhof
Maj. Edward Galvin
Sally Gardner
Warren E. Gardner, Jr.
Luise Greiner
Georgia Herrick
Audrey Hoffman
Walter Karpowich
Lt. William Lovelock
Nancy Maginnes
Ronald Maiorana
Arthur Mann
Hugh Morrow
Mary Nestor
Maxine Paul
Martha Plummer
Hailey Rodwell
Nancy Shea
Bert Smith
Walter Thompson
Marshall Watzke
Ann C. Whitman

Special Acknowledgment for Counsel and Advice on the Preparation of the Report to the President:

Hugh Morrow
Oscar M. Ruebhausen
James M. Cannon
Alan D. Miller, M.D.

FOREWORD

The following report and recommendations are the outgrowth of what the members of the mission learned in discussions with more than three thousand leaders of the twenty countries which the mission visited.

We found in the course of our travels and talks that our perspective concerning the nations we visited and the hopes of their people was more meaningful when taken in the context of the entire Western Hemisphere. The quality of life in one area of the hemisphere is inseparably linked with all the rest. Moreover, if we do not meet the fundamental needs of our own people at home, we cannot expect to inspire or assist the people of other nations to meet their own needs. The more we understood the situation in the other republics, the more clearly we understood what was happening at home—and the more we appreciated the need for unity of the hemisphere.

We have, accordingly, in this report looked at the challenges and opportunities from the point of view of the hemisphere as a whole. Because of this, we have written this report with the hope that Canada might join with all the American republics in a truly hemisphere response to what are in fact common concerns. We were also moved by the hope that one day Cuba can be restored to the society of free men.

These trips were an enriching experience. To convey some sense of our personal reactions, as a group, to this fruitful opportunity to listen to the responsible people in South and Central America and the Caribbean, a Preamble is included in our report.

N.A.R.

PREAMBLE

We went to visit neighbors and found brothers. We went to listen to the spokesmen of our sister republics and heard the voices of a hemisphere.

We went to annotate, to document, and to record. We did so; and we also learned, grew, and changed.

We used the tools of specialists: economists and scientists, artists and architects, agronomists and social workers. But there is not one of us who did not reappraise the uses of his specialty, who did not find his sense of purpose and values renewed.

We thought to study the ways of life in the other American nations, to measure their performance and ours. We rediscovered the quality of life for each person in the hemisphere, and finally the world, as the only measure of lasting consequence.

Our country was born and has experienced the greatest flowering of human capacities in all recorded time because one great idea was unloosed. And though many neglect it, and others would suppress it, it has not yet been contained: the noble concept that each person is the reason and each person is the strength for the nation.

In the release of our collective energies, we have produced great systems and organizations, techniques of awesome capabilities, and a mosaic of useful things and objects here in the United States. But we have lost sight of the values which are the real source of our greatness. We have exported our systems, techniques, and objects, but their distribution has not been essentially shaped by the values that inspired our nation at home—nor have we transmitted those values.

In the countries we visited, we had the opportunity to see ourselves through their eyes. Even allowing for the distortions of distance and the biases of incomplete knowledge, one theme resounded throughout the hemisphere: you the people of the United States are strong and you are able, but you lack unifying goals and a clear sense of national purpose.

In our concentrated exposure to twenty nations, during thousands of hours of discussions for which our hosts had painstakingly prepared, during planned and unplanned encounters, in the presence of both hospitality and hostility, our group had a dual experience.

We were given a great deal of information about the many dimensions of life in this hemisphere. We exchanged points of view on mutual problems and explored possible solutions. And we have together formed new hypotheses and found new techniques in the many special areas of our concern.

We have also come to one simple principle and it shapes our report: All that we have seen, all that we think that we understand, all that we will recommend must be tested against the single question—how does this affect the way that men live?

The logistics of travel and work had determined our itinerary. Thus each week of our visits was followed by a week at home. Among us, we live in all quarters of the United States and work in many different situations. This repeated alternation may have contributed to a conviction that grew among us: the variations among all people are our great common wealth; and we share the same human problems.

As individuals and as nations, we must learn from one another, and we need constant collaboration and communication with each other if our species is to thrive—or even to survive.

It is for each individual, each family, each community, each nation, each region to define its own particular aspirations—but these share one splendid bias: that no man be exploited or degraded to enrich another, and that we work together so that each can grow.

Some nations have moved further toward this goal than others, but all nations, including our own, have more to grow than they have grown and more to do than they have done.

This aspiration, when truly applied, has a hard, fine cutting edge. We must ask what necessary elements must come together, in and around each person, if he is to live and grow. Opportunity for self-realization comes immediately to mind—the chance to grow spiritually, the respect for human dignity and justice, the right to hope that life will get better, not worse. Certain commodities, physical circumstances, material requirements also come to mind. Comfort and safety amidst the changing elements: shelter and clothing. Energy: enough of the necessary kinds of food, water. Safety from violence and intrusion upon privacy, and an environment sufficiently free of noxious influence.

But man is a social, learning, creative, responsible, and self-aware creature, and he needs—absolutely requires—much more if he is to thrive, to become more fully himself. He needs the ability and freedom to move, the opportunities to learn and contribute, to ornament and create, to share his experiences and his hopes. He needs to be able to influence the forces which impinge upon him, to participate in his own destiny, and to be recognized for his own accomplishments.

There is in none of this the blandishment of easy or final success. Even our expanding horizons have limits, substance and energy are finite, hard choices must be made again and again. We are a species that is both giving and acquisitive, creative and indolent, gentle and violent, petty and magnificent. But when we choose, when we commit our energies to a common goal, none yet has been beyond us.

We face today a crisis in human expectations. Individuals and nations expect much for themselves and too little for others. But expectations are powerful moving forces. They change the ways people act. The very anticipation that it is more natural to take than to give, consume than to create, tends to fulfill itself. It is urgent that we acknowledge in all peoples the same capacities for giving and sharing that we ascribe to ourselves.

Each country in the Western Hemisphere has its own special history and tradition, and forms of government which do not give the same kind of recognition to individuals. Neither do individuals in each of our nations regard their social obligations in the same fashion. But it is a basic assumption of this mission that men are more alike than otherwise in their potential for social responsiveness, and that latent in our species and in each of us is a capacity for personal growth through an enlarged concern for others.

The urgent human problems in the Western Hemisphere require that the nations help one another. At the least, the patterns of our cooperation and mutual assistance should reflect the expectation that all of us will move toward broadly participating governmental systems which represent the interests of each citizen. If we couple this expectation with an appreciation for the work and steps that must be undertaken to reach this goal, and for the difficulties in change, we will have embarked on a new direction in which we all begin to raise each other up.

CHAPTER ONE

THE QUALITY OF LIFE IN THE WESTERN HEMISPHERE

A. The Special Relationship in the Western Hemisphere

The mission heard many details about the relations between the United States and the other American republics from the leaders of the hemisphere, but they can best be summed up in one sentence: The United States has allowed the special relationship it has historically maintained with the other nations of the Western Hemisphere to deteriorate badly.

The United States has allowed a host of narrow special interests, a series of other foreign policy priorities, budgetary and balance of payments constraints, a burgeoning bureaucratic tangle, and well-intentioned but unrealistic rhetoric to submerge this special relationship to the point where many of its neighbors in the hemisphere wonder if the United States really does care. Its assistance and trade policies, so critical to the development process of other nations, have been distorted to serve a variety of purposes in the United States having nothing to do with the aspirations and interests of its neighbors; in fact, all too often these purposes have been in sharp conflict with the goals of development.

Moreover, in its relations, the United States has all too often demonstrated, at least subconsciously, a paternalistic attitude toward the other nations of the hemisphere. It has tried to direct the internal affairs of other nations to an unseemly degree, thinking, perhaps arrogantly, that it knew what was best for them. It has underestimated the capacities of these nations and their willingness to assume responsibility for the course of future developments. The United States has talked about partnership, but it has not truly practiced it.

At the same time, we found that profound changes are occurring in the hemisphere, changes that have not been fully understood. It is clear that these changes will affect all of us, and that we must get rid of some of our stereotypes and conditioned thinking if we are to understand and respond with intelligence and pragmatism to the forces of change.

We have concluded that the national interest requires the United States to revive its special relationship with the nations of the hemisphere, and that this relationship should be reinvigorated with a new commitment, new forms, and new style. Western Hemisphere relationships cannot remain static; the forces of change—and our own best interests as well as those of the entire hemisphere—will not permit it.

This report tries to understand some of the issues we must face in attempting to reinvigorate and reshape our special relationship—and it offers some specific recommendations for action now.

B. The Existing Situation

Everywhere in the Western Hemisphere today, including the United States, men and women are enjoying a fuller life, but still for many the realities of life are in sharp contrast with the deepest felt human needs and goals of the people.

Everywhere in the hemisphere we see similar problems—problems of population and poverty, urbanization and unemployment, illiteracy and injustice, violence and disorder.

Although each of the twenty-six countries in the hemisphere is different, with widely varying stages of development, aspirations are outrunning resources and accomplishments everywhere. All nations of the hemisphere share rising expectations and restlessness among those men and women who do not truly participate in the benefits of the industrial revolution and the standard of living which has come with it.

Even among some who have shared in the benefits, there is an increasing tendency to lose confidence and sureness of purpose. This makes fertile soil for the ever-present disruptive forces ready to exploit those who are uncertain and to stir up those who are restless.

We know from our experience in the United States that

those who live in deprived circumstances no longer live out of sight and out of mind. Neither are they resigned—nor should they be resigned—to the fact that their lives are less than they could be.

They have looked at the relative quality of their life and found it wanting.

As a result, in the United States and throughout the Western Hemisphere, the legitimacy of the democratic political system and the individual enterprise economic system are under challenge.

The upheavals in international systems over the past three decades have subjected the member states of the Western Hemisphere to external economic, political, and ideological stresses that magnify domestic antagonisms.

At the same time, the issue of political legitimacy has challenged "accepted" systems of government, not only in the United States but particularly in the other American republics. With the disintegration of old orders which lacked a popular base, newly emerging domestic structures have had difficulty in establishing their legitimacy. This makes the problem of creating a system of political order in the Western Hemisphere more difficult.

Some nations have retained their democratic institutions. In others, when democratic forms of government have not been successful, nations have moved to authoritarian forms as a solution to political and social dilemmas. Governments everywhere are struggling to cope with often conflicting demands for social reform and economic growth. The problem is compounded by the four-hundred-year-old heritage of intense individualism which permeates all phases of life in the Latin countries of the Americas. Nationalism is burgeoning in most of the region with strong anti–United States overtones. Increasing frustration is evidenced over political instability, limited educational and economic opportunities, and the incapacity or slowness of existing government structures to solve the people's problems. Subversive forces working throughout the hemisphere are quick to exploit and exacerbate each and every situation.

Change and the stresses and problems brought about by the processes of change characterize the existing situation in the hemisphere. The momentum of industrialization and modernization has strained the fabric of social and political structures. Political and social instability, increased pressure for radical answers to the problems, and a growing tendency to nationalistic independence from the United States dominate the setting.

The restless yearning of individuals for a better life, particularly when accompanied by a well-developed sense of social responsibility, is chipping away at the very order and institutions by which society makes it possible for man to fulfill his personal dignity. The seeds of nihilism and anarchy are spreading throughout the hemisphere.

C. The Forces of Change

Change is the crucial characteristic of our time. It is erupting, and disrupting, in all cultures. It creates anxiety and uncertainty. It is demanding of all peoples an adjustment and flexibility which test the limits of individual and collective capacities.

Change is everywhere about us: in the explosion of new knowledge, the acceleration of all communication, the massive mobility of people, the multiplicity of human contacts, the pace and diversity of experience, the increasingly transitory nature of all relationships, and the uprooting of the values to which differing cultures are anchored.

There is no society today, whether industrialized or developing, that is not coping with these hurricane forces of change. It is plain that, depending on how we respond to the need for change and the demands of these forces, the results can be tremendously constructive or tremendously destructive.

The sweeping change occurring in the hemisphere will affect our interests and our relationships with the other nations of the hemisphere. We must recognize that the United States cannot control the forces of change. However, we can and must try to *understand* the forces at work in the hemisphere—as well as at home—and how they may affect our national interests if we are to shape intelligently and realistically our relationships.

Throughout the hemisphere, although people are constantly

moving out of poverty and degradation in varying numbers, the gap between the advantaged and the disadvantaged, within nations as well as between nations, is ever sharper and ever more difficult to endure. It is made to seem all the worse by the facility of modern communications.

Communications

The transistor radio has brought about a revolution in awareness. Millions who used to be isolated by illiteracy and remote location now know that there is a different way of life which others are privileged to enjoy. Never again will they be content to accept as inevitable the patterns of the past. They want to share the privileges of progress. They want a better world for their children. They have listened too long to unfulfilled promises. Their expectations have outrun performance. Their frustration is turning to a growing sense of injustice and disillusionment.

Science and Technology

Science and technology have not, however, kept pace with communications in the developing nations of the Western Hemisphere. These nations have lagged seriously in their participation in the scientific and cultural revolution which has been an essential part of the industrialization of the developed nations. Many American republics have not, therefore, shared proportionately in the increased productivity and rising standards of living of their northern neighbors. This has fanned the flames of jealousy, resentment, and frustration.

Most of the American republics have not yet mobilized the necessary elements for widespread industrialization of their economies. They need, in varying degrees, more and better education, more effective systems for channeling national savings into capital formation and industrial investment, laws to protect the public's interests while encouraging the spirit of entrepreneurship, and expanding governmental services to support industrial growth.

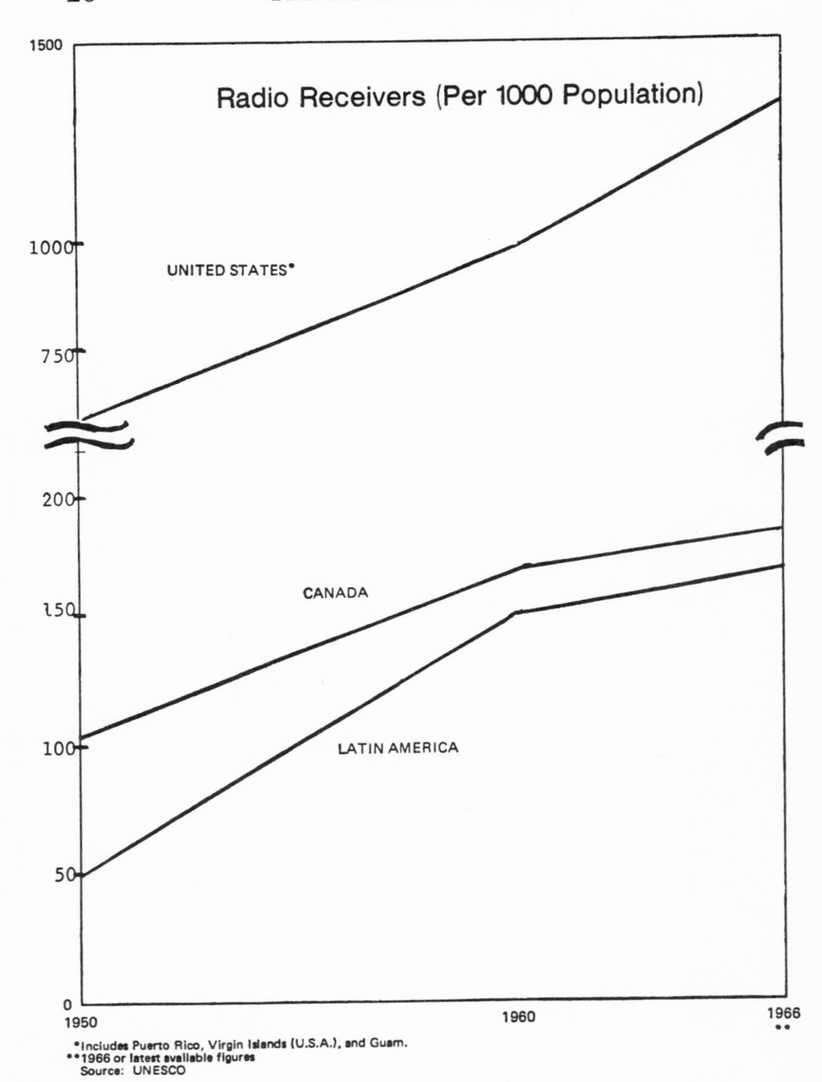

The Revolution in Communications Has Brought About a Revolution in Awareness.

Population Growth

Another vital force for change is the fact that the population of most American republics is the fastest-growing in the world.

PERCENT INCREASE OF POPULATION DURING TEN-YEAR PERIODS

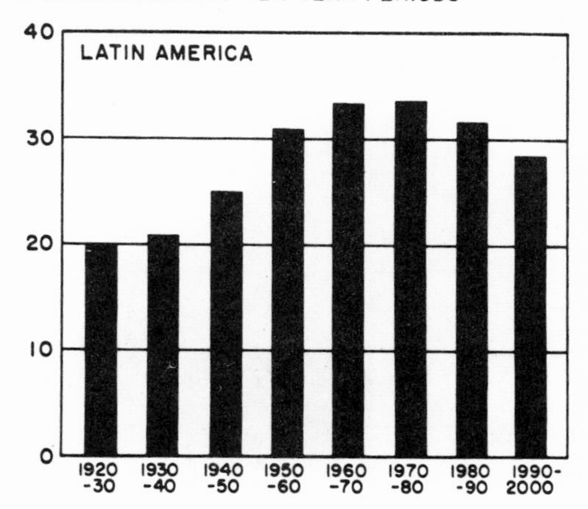

Source: U.N., World Population Prospects

The fact that over 60 per cent of the population is now under twenty-four years of age has greatly increased the demands on government for more schools, more health services, more housing and roads—services beyond their resources to provide. It produces an increasing labor supply which cannot find enough work, and thus adds to frustrations and tensions. It results in slum growth and a multiplication of the problems of urban life, and it cancels out so much of the economic growth achieved as to make improvement of living standards difficult if not impossible.

Urban Life

With urbanization in the Western Hemisphere have come crowded living conditions and a loss of living space in physical and psychological terms. The urban man tends to become both depersonalized and fragmented in his human relation-

PERCENTAGE OF POPULATION BY AGE*

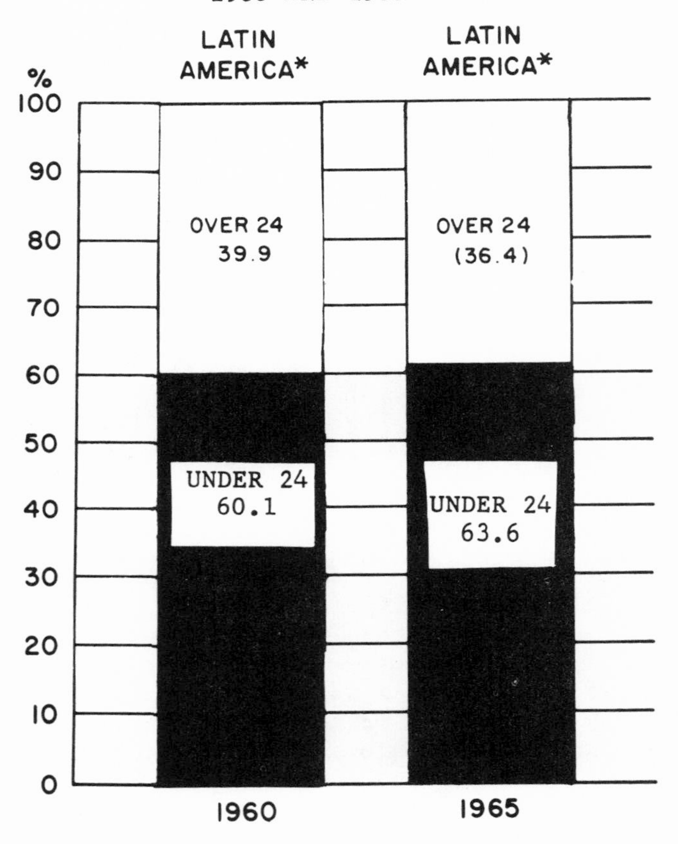

*Includes Caribbean SOURCE: UNESCO

ships. Unemployment is high, especially among the young, ranging as high as 25 to 40 per cent in some countries—and as low as 4 per cent in others. The impact of poverty is widespread. These sprawling urban areas of the hemisphere spawn restlessness and anger which are readily exploited by the varying forces that thrive on trouble—and such forces are present in all societies.

The problems of urbanization are multiplied by an increasing migration to the cities of the rural poor, who are least prepared for the stresses of industrial urban society.

One positive force is the political emergence of women. They now have the right to vote in every country of the hemisphere—and are proving to be, by and large, a middle-of-the-road influence.

Nationalism

All of this is heightened by the spirit of nationalism which has been an essential element in the emotional makeup of all the American republics since their independence. The curve of nationalist sentiment is generally rising as these societies strive toward greater national identity and self-assertiveness. Since the United States looms so large in the lives of the other nations, and its power and presence is so overwhelming, this nationalism tends more and more to find the United States a tempting and natural target.

Nationalism is not confined to any one country, nor does it spring from any one source. Political and pressure groups of all persuasions lean heavily on the exploitation of nationalistic sentiment.

This national sensitivity has been fed by the fact that, in the other American republics, United States management, capital, and highly advertised products have played a disproportionately visible role. A high percentage of overseas investment has come from the United States, principally to seek raw materials or to preserve markets.

The forces of nationalism are creating increasing pressures against foreign private investment. The impetus for independence from the United States is leading toward rising pressures for nationalization of U.S. industry, local control, or participation with U.S. firms. Most economists and businessmen in the other American republics recognize the clear need for U.S. capital and technology, but they want them on terms consistent with their desire for self-determination.

Thus the rising drive for self-identification is naturally and inevitably leading many nations to seek greater independence from U.S. influence and power. The dilemma posed for the governments is that they know that U.S. cooperation and participation can contribute greatly to accelerating achievement of their development goals, but their sense of political legitimacy may well depend on the degree of independence they can maintain from the United States.

YOUNG PEOPLE

In view of current conditions, it is natural that growing numbers of people in nations throughout the hemisphere, including the United States, should be disillusioned with society's failures—and perturbed by a sense of loss of individual identity.

Increasing numbers of young people especially are questioning many of our basic premises. They are searching for new values, new meanings, new importance for the individual's worth and dignity.

Student participation in demonstrations and violence is becoming a major force in all countries. This is so regardless of political ideology, regardless of whether the students are acting spontaneously or have been organized. Man has demonstrated in the past that he can endure regimentation; the test today, perhaps, is whether he can survive his freedom.

The idealism of youth is and should be one of the most promising forces for the future. At the same time, the very fact of their idealism makes some of the young vulnerable to subversive penetration and to exploitation as a revolutionary means for the destruction of the existing order. Above all, it is clear that the young people of the hemisphere will no longer accept slogans as substitutes for solutions. They know a better life is possible.

LABOR

Yet it is not only the young who are deeply concerned or seeking instant fulfillment of their aspirations. The same phenomena are present in the ranks of labor. The largest groups in the developing labor movement throughout the hemisphere have democratic leadership. They seek increased productivity for their nations and a fair share of that increased productivity for the workers and their families. But a substantial segment of labor is communist-led—and less concerned with the nation's productivity than with the overthrow of existing institutions, public and private.

The Cross and the Sword

Although it is not yet widely recognized, the military establishments and the Catholic Church are also among today's forces for social and political change in the other American republics. This is a new role for them. For since the arrival of the Conquistadores more than four hundred years ago, the history of the military and the Catholic Church, working hand in hand with the landowners to provide "stability," has been a legend in the Americas.

Few people realize the extent to which both these institutions are now breaking with their pasts. They are, in fact, moving rapidly to the forefront as forces for social, economic, and political change. In the case of the Church, this is a recognition of a need to be more responsive to the popular will. In the case of the military, it is a reflection of a broadening of opportunities for young men regardless of family background.

The Church

Modern communications and increasing education have brought about a stirring among the people that has had a tremendous impact on the Church,* making it a force dedicated to change—revolutionary change if necessary.

Actually, the Church may be somewhat in the same situation as the young—with a profound idealism, but as a result, in some cases, vulnerable to subversive penetration; ready to undertake a revolution if necessary to end injustice, but not clear either as to the ultimate nature of the revolution itself or as to the governmental system by which the justice it seeks can be realized.

* See documents prepared by the Second General Conference of the Latin American Roman Catholic Episcopate in Medellín, Colombia, in 1968.

THE MILITARY

In many South and Central American countries, the military is the single most powerful political group in society. Military men are symbols of power, authority, and sovereignty and a focus of national pride. They have traditionally been regarded in most countries as the ultimate arbiters of the nation's welfare.

The tendency of the military to intervene when it judges that the government in office has failed to carry out its responsibilities properly has generally been accepted in Central and South America. Virtually all military governments in the hemisphere have assumed power to "rescue" the country from an incompetent government, or an intolerable economic or political situation. Historically, these regimes have varied widely in their attitudes toward civil liberties, social reform, and repression.

Like the Church, the military was traditionally a conservative force resistant to change. Most officers came from the landowner class. In recent years, however, the owners of land have shifted more and more to an urban industrial life. The military service has been less attractive to their sons. As a result, opportunities have opened up for young men of ambition and ability from poor families who have neither land nor professional and business connections. These ambitious sons of the working classes have entered the military to seek an education and the opportunity for advancement.

This pattern has become almost universal throughout the American republics to the south. The ablest of these young officers have gone abroad for education and are now assuming top positions of leadership in almost all of the military groups in the hemisphere. And while their loyalties are with the armed forces, their emotional ties are often with the people. Increasingly, their concern and dedication is to the eradication of poverty and the improvement of the lot of the oppressed, both in rural and urban areas.

In short, a new type of military man is coming to the fore and often becoming a major force for constructive social change in the American republics. Motivated by increasing impatience with corruption, inefficiency, and a stagnant political order, the new military man is prepared to adapt his authoritarian tradition to the goals of social and economic progress.

This new role by the military, however, is not free from perils and dilemmas. There is always the risk that the authoritarian style will result in represson. The temptation to expand measures for security or discipline or efficiency to the point of curtailing individual liberties, beyond what is required for the restoration of order and social progress, is not easy to resist.

Above all, authoritarian governments, bent on rapid change, have an intrinsic ideological unreliability and a vulnerability to extreme nationalism. They can go in almost any doctrinal direction.

The danger for the new military is that it may become isolated from the people with authoritarianism turning into a means to suppress rather than eliminate the buildup of social and political tension.

The critical test, ultimately, is whether the new military can and will move the nation, with sensitivity and conscious design, toward a transition from military control for a social purpose to a more pluralistic form of government which will enable individual talent and dignity to flourish. Or will they become radicalized, statist, and anti-U.S.?

In this connection, special mention should be made of the appeal to the new military, on a theoretical level, of Marxism: (1) it justifies, through its elitist-vanguard theories, government by a relatively small group or single institution (such as the Army) and, at the same time, (2) produces a rationale for state-enforced sacrifices to further economic development.

One important influence counteracting this simplistic Marxist approach is the exposure to the fundamental achievements of the U.S. way of life that many of the military from the other American countries have received through the military training programs which the U.S. conducts in Panama and the United States.

Business

A similar phenomenon is apparent within the business community. Again, there is a dichotomy. On the one hand, long-established self-interests cling to practices of paternalism and monopoly behind high protective tariffs. On the other hand, new enterprises or older businesses with new, young management are bringing to bear a social concern for workers and the public as well as for stockholders.

This new business leadership is a promising and constructive force. And it is a necessary force in the process of change, simply because the technical, managerial, and marketing competence of private business must assume a major role in the development of the Western Hemisphere.

COMMUNIST SUBVERSION

In every country there is a restless striving for a better life. Coming as it does at a time of uprooting change, it brings to many a vague unease that all the systems of society are out of control. In such a setting, all of the American nations are a tempting target for communist subversion. In fact, it is plainly evident that such subversion is a reality today with alarming potential.

Castro has consistently recruited from the other American republics, and trained in Cuba, guerrillas to export the Cuban-type communist agrarian revolution. Fortunately, the governments of the American republics have gradually improved their capabilities for dealing with Castro-type agrarian guerrillas. However, radical revolutionary elements in the hemisphere appear to be increasingly turning toward urban terrorism in their attempts to bring down the existing order. This type of subversion is more difficult to control, and governments are forced to use increasingly repressive measures to deal with it. Thus, a cycle of terrorist actions and repressive counter-reactions tend to polarize and unsettle the political situation, creating more fertile ground for radical solutions among large segments of the population.

There are also Maoist Communist forces in the hemisphere. Although they are relatively small in numbers they are fanatically dedicated to the use of violence and intimidation to achieve their ends. The mystique of Maoism has appealed most to the idealism of the young and thus has been the means for widespread subversion.

Now it appears in some cases that Castro and Maoist forces have joined for acts of subversion, terror, and violence in the cities. These forces also concentrate on mass student demonstrations and disruptions of various institutions, public and private, calling on the support of communist labor-front organizations to the degree possible.

Although Castro's propaganda casts him as a leader of the downtrodden who is opposed to United States imperialism and independent of Soviet communism, it is clear that the Soviet Union presently has an important degree of financial, economic, and military influence over Communist Cuba. The recent visit of the Soviet fleet to Havana is one evidence of growing warmth in their relations.

This Soviet performance in Cuba and throughout the hemisphere is to be contrasted to the official Soviet government and Communist party protestations not only of peaceful coexistence but of disassociation from Castro and his program of terror in the American republics.

Clearly, the opinion in the United States that communism is no longer a serious factor in the Western Hemisphere is thoroughly wrong.

We found almost universally that the other American republics are deeply concerned about the threat that it poses to them—and the United States must be alert to and concerned about the ultimate threat it poses to the United States and the hemisphere as a whole.

Changes in the Decade Ahead

The nations of the Western Hemisphere in the decade ahead will differ greatly from their present situation. They will reflect the rapid and widespread changes now occurring, which will alter the institutions and processes by which the American republics govern and progress. While it is not possible to predict with any precision the precise course of change, the hemisphere is likely to exhibit the following characteristics in the next few years:

—Rising frustration with the pace of development, intensified by industrialization, urbanization, and population growth;

—Political and social instability;

—An increased tendency to turn to authoritarian or radical solutions;

—Continuation of the trend of the military to take power for the purpose of guiding social and economic progress; and,

—Growing nationalism, across the spectrum of political groupings, which will often find expression in terms of independence from U.S. domination and influence.

CHAPTER TWO

THE CHALLENGE TO POLITICAL AND ECONOMIC FREEDOM

A. The Nature of the Challenge

The pace and intensity of change, imposed on rampant inflation, urban violence, grinding poverty, embittering injustice, and flaming nationalism, put the nations of the Western Hemisphere at a crossroads. The question of whether systems of freedom with order and justice will survive and prosper is no longer rhetorical; it is reality.

The key issue is whether government of free peoples can be made effective, and can set the necessary priorities, to cope with the people's present needs and their aspirations for the future; whether political and social institutions can hold the confidence not only of a questioning young generation but of adults as well.

For the United States, the challenge is a double one: first, to demonstrate by its example that a free society can resolve its own internal problems and provide a more rewarding life for all its people; second, to find ways in which its tremendous human and material resources can effectively supplement the efforts of the other American nations themselves, in a climate of growing instability, extremism, and anti-U.S. nationalism.

A new relationship between the United States and the other American republics must be shaped with a recognition that devotion to our long-term community of interests will often require sensitive handling of our short-term differences. In forging this relationship we have the opportunity to demonstrate how sovereign nations, working together, can solve common problems and thus to establish a model for cooperative arrangements for the fulfillment of men and women throughout the world.

It is a fortunate and striking fact of the modern world that, for the first time, the scientific know-how and managerial competence required to meet the economic aspects of the challenge are available. Moreover, we believe the Western Hemisphere possesses the human, material, and spiritual resources that are needed for the task in all its aspects—economic, social, and political.

B. The United States' National Interest

The moral and spiritual strength of the United States in the world, the political credibility of our leadership, the security of our nation, the future of our social and economic lives are now at stake.

Rising frustrations throughout the Western Hemisphere over poverty and political instability have led increasing numbers of people to pick the United States as a scapegoat and to seek out Marxist solutions to their socio-economic problems. At the moment, there is only one Castro among the twenty-six nations of the hemisphere; there can well be more in the future. And a Castro on the mainland, supported militarily and economically by the communist world, would present the gravest kind of threat to the security of the Western Hemisphere and pose an extremely difficult problem for the United States.

Just as the other American republics depend upon the United States for their capital equipment requirements, so the United States depends on them to provide a vast market for our manufactured goods. And as these countries look to the United States for a market for their primary products whose sale enables them to buy equipment for their development at home, so the United States looks to them for raw materials for our industries, on which depend the jobs of many of our citizens.

But these forces of economic interdependence are changing, and must change. An increasing flow of two-way trade in industrial products must supplement the present interchange of manufactured goods and primary products.

Today's 250 million people in South and Central America will become 643 million in just thirty years. If the current anti-U.S. trend continues, one can foresee a time when the United States would be politically and morally isolated from part or much of the Western Hemisphere. If this should happen, the barriers to our collective growth would become formidable indeed.

It is plainly evident that the countries of the Western Hemisphere, including the United States, have become increasingly dependent on each other.

Historically, the United States has had a special relationship with the other American republics. It is based upon long association, geography, and, above all, on the psychological acceptance of a concept of hemisphere community. It is embodied in the web of organizations, treaties, and commitments of the inter-American system. Beyond conventional security and economic interests, the political and psychological value of the special relationship cannot be overestimated. Failure to maintain that special relationship would imply a failure of our capacity and responsibility as a great power. If we cannot maintain a constructive relationship in the Western Hemisphere, we will hardly be able to achieve a successful order elsewhere in the world. Moreover, failure to maintain the special relationship would create a vacuum in the hemisphere and facilitate the influence in the region of hostile foreign powers.

It is clear, then, that our national interest requires the maintenance of our special relationship which should have as its goal the creation of a community of self-reliant, independent nations linked in a mutually beneficial regional system, and seeking to improve the efficiency of their societies and the quality of life of their peoples.

C. Our National Objective

There is no system in all of history better than our own flexible structure of political democracy, individual initiative, and responsible citizenship in elevating the quality of man's life. It makes the individual of central importance; it subordinates the role of government as a servant of the people; it works with people and for people—it has no other justification.

Our job at home is far from finished. We must keep our emphasis on people, our priority concern for people. This will mean shaping the forces of change and stretching out or deferring those programs not related to the urgent needs of people. Unless human needs are met, democracy will have failed of its purpose and cannot survive.

What is true at home is essentially also true for the hemisphere. Our concern must be for people. What we in the hemisphere have to do is work together, multiplying our relations with the people of the hemisphere nations, helping each other develop more effective societies that can enhance the health, freedom, and security of all the people, to the end that the quality of the life of each and every person in the hemisphere is enhanced.

We must work with our fellow Americans to the end that no one is exploited or degraded to enrich another, and every man and woman has a full opportunity to make the most of his endowments.

However, we must recognize that the specific forms or processes by which each nation moves toward a pluralistic system will vary with its own traditions and situation. We know that we, in the United States, cannot determine the internal political structure of any other nation, except by example.

Our ability to affect or influence the course of events in other nations is limited. We may find that other nations may perceive their interests in ways which conflict with ours. What we must do is take a long-term view of our interests and objectives, always maintaining a sense of our own priorities and of the special Western Hemisphere relationship we hope to achieve. Such a view will require a high degree of tolerance for diversity and for nationalistic expression often directed against the United States, and a recognition that our style may often have a more important effect than what we actually do in the hemisphere.

The kind of paternalistic relationship the United States has had in the past with other hemisphere nations will be increasingly costly and counter-productive in the years ahead. We believe the United States must move increasingly toward a relationship of true partnership, in which it will cooperate with other nations of the hemisphere in those areas where its cooperation can be helpful and is wanted.

The United States must face several important practical issues in trying to shape this new relationship:

1. The United States should determine its attitude toward internal political developments in a more pragmatic way;
2. The United States should decide how it can shift increasing responsibility to the other American nations (through multi-lateral channels) for the development process; and,
3. The United States should decide how its interests are affected by insurgency and subversion elsewhere in the hemisphere and the extent to which its programs can and should assist in meeting the security requirements of its neighbors.

The task is difficult but by no means impossible. It will require discipline and energy and, above all, a very clear and consistent sense of purpose at home and abroad. To grasp the opportunity that lies in the hemisphere, the United States must make some major and fundamental changes in, first, the structure of government mechanisms through which we work with our hemisphere neighbors, and, second, in our policies and programs as they relate to the Western Hemisphere.

Accordingly, Chapters Three and Four of this report will make specific recommendations in each of the areas: first, organization, and, second, policy.

CHAPTER THREE

ORGANIZATION

A. Organization of the United States Government

Unless there is a major reorganization of the United States government structure, with clear lines of responsibility and corresponding authority to make policy and direct operations in the Western Hemisphere, the effect of other recommendations would, at best, be marginal.

Under the Constitution, the President has the responsibility for the formulation and execution of foreign policy. Where there are conflicting interests and points of view among the government departments and agencies, only the President has the authority to reconcile the differences and make the decisions.

With the present United States government structure, Western Hemisphere policy can neither be soundly formulated nor effectively carried out.

Contrary to popular misconceptions, the State Department does not have effective overall responsibility for foreign policy where the interests of other departments of the government are concerned. In actual fact, the State Department controls less than half the policy decisions directly relating to the Western Hemisphere. Responsibility for policy and operations is scattered among many departments and agencies—for example, Treasury, Commerce, Agriculture, and Defense.

To cope with the diffusion of authority, there has grown up a complex and cumbersome system of interdepartmental committees within which there are interminable negotiations because no one member has the authority to make a final decision. The result is that there are endless delays in decision-making. Too often, agreement is reached on major subjects only by compromise in the lower echelons of government—often at the lowest common denominator of agreement.

The result is that we have no clear formulation of United States policy objectives toward the Western Hemisphere. Nor are there clear policy guidelines relating to substantive and regional problems which are essential to effective day-to-day decision-making in our contacts with the other American republics. This in itself leads to conflicts within the government which are detrimental to the best interests of our country.

In this maze of bureaucracy and procrastination, the representatives of the Western Hemisphere governments become frustrated and humiliated because they are referred from one department to another without finding anyone who can make a final decision. Delays in Washington of months and even years on decisions of major importance to their countries were reported to the mission in almost every nation we visited.

The lack of clear policy direction, the indecision, and the resulting frustration are major factors in preventing the kind of understanding and close working relationships which are essential in light of our growing interdependence.

Obviously, neither the President nor the Secretary of State has the time for continuing attention to the concern of twenty-five other nations in the hemisphere, and no one else has the authority. As a result, the day-to-day relationships with our friends and neighbors, including Canada, do not get the constant consideration of our top policy-makers.

But if we are to have a true sense of community within the Western Hemisphere, it must be possible to establish and maintain high-level contacts with each country on a basis of frankness and openness that will minimize the danger of misunderstanding and maximize effective cooperation. Such cooperation depends on the ability of the United States to respond promptly and decisively. For the United States to organize itself to make this possible:

1. There must be clearly defined national objectives consistent with the goals of the Western Hemisphere community;
2. These objectives must be translated into clear policy positions relating to both governmental and private activities;
3. To implement these national goals and policies effectively, there must be a structure with clear lines of responsibility and authority flowing directly from the President;

4. There must be efficiently run organizations that can carry out supporting programs free from political and diplomatic encumbrances which reduce the effectiveness of technical and professional operations; and,

5. There must be a close working relationship with the members of Congress as an indispensable and integral part of the policy-making process.

Finally, and of overriding importance in our special Western Hemisphere relationships, is the psychological factor of personal relationships, so important to the Latins.

A characteristic of the Latin temperament is to put more faith in people than in institutions. It therefore is important to give stature and dignity to the key position of leadership in the structure of the United States government that deals with the Western Hemisphere. One man should symbolize, by the importance of his position, the President's special interest in and concern for our Western Hemisphere relations. Creation of such a post must therefore outweigh any traditional objections to a change of government organization.

In this way, we can establish a sense of vitality, openness, and effectiveness in our relations with the leaders and peoples of the other nations. This is essential to the unity and security of the Western Hemisphere and will make possible the achievement of our common goals.

Recommendation: National Policy Objective

The President should reorganize the foreign policy and operating structure of United States government dealing with the Western Hemisphere.

Recommendations for Action

1. *A* Secretary of Western Hemisphere Affairs *should be created to give day-to-day leadership and guidance on behalf of the Secretary of State and the President. He would also coordinate on their behalf all United States government activities in the Western Hemisphere.*
   a. He would be the focal point within the United States government of all matters pertaining to Western

Hemisphere affairs, subject to the President and the Secretary of State.

b. He would have the authority and responsibility to represent the President and the Secretary of State in negotiations with chiefs of state, foreign ministers, and other senior officials of hemisphere nations, and with heads of all United States government departments and agencies concerned with hemisphere policy and operations.

c. He would be supported by Undersecretaries for Western Hemisphere economic and political affairs, and appropriate Assistant Secretaries, including one for each regional trading group of nations.

2. *There should be created within the National Security Council a* WESTERN HEMISPHERE POLICY STAFF DIRECTOR *to service the President, the National Security Council, the Secretary of State, the Secretary of Western Hemisphere Affairs, and the various departments and agencies involved, such as Defense, Treasury, Commerce, and Agriculture, and economic and social program activities.*

a. The Director would serve the Assistant to the President for National Security Affairs and would thus have experts with competence in the fields represented by the key departments and agencies involved in Western Hemisphere affairs.

b. The purpose of this White House staff would be to help in the formulation of the President's Western Hemisphere goals and policies in consultation with the appropriate councils of government.

c. It would monitor Executive Office decisions relating to the Western Hemisphere through the departments, agencies, and beyond to determine whether presidential decisions are being carried out.

3. *An* ECONOMIC AND SOCIAL DEVELOPMENT AGENCY *should be created in the Executive Office of the President to supersede the present AID administration in the State Department. This move is essential for a number of reasons:*

a. The financial and technical operations of the State Department have gotten all tangled up with the diplomatic responsibilities of the State Department—to the detriment of both.

b. Because of the lack of clear administrative responsibility and authority in the AID organization, it is having great difficulty in recruiting quality staff.
c. Economic assistance policy operating decisions are too often made on the basis of political negotiations rather than economic and social realities.
d. Under the proposed structure, the new Development Agency would have clear lines of authority from the President but would have to clear its operating programs with the appropriate policy officials in the State Department.

4. *An* INSTITUTE OF WESTERN HEMISPHERE AFFAIRS *should be set up under the Development Agency as the operating corporation to carry out government-to-government economic and social programs in the Western Hemisphere.*
   a. The activities of this Western Hemisphere corporate institute would be subject to the President, the Secretary of Western Hemisphere Affairs (on behalf of the Secretary of State), and the Policy Staff Director of the Security Council.
   b. Clearance of operating programs would be accomplished by the following procedure:
      —A concise project memo would be prepared and, when it related to a Western Hemisphere nation, it would be submitted to the Secretary of Western Hemisphere Affairs for his political approval. In each case, the memo would clearly state the objectives of the project, its nature and character, the number of people to be employed, and the total cost.
      —After the project had been cleared by the Secretary of Western Hemisphere Affairs, he would inform the United States ambassador in the country involved—and instruct him to support the carrying-out of the project. If, at any time, the ambassador felt that the project was in any way prejudicial to the best interests of the United States, he would first take the matter up with the director of the project; failing satisfaction there, he would report his complaint to the Secretary of Western Hemisphere Affairs who,

in turn, would take it up with the head of either the assistance program or the regional functional institute responsible for its execution.

c. Creation of the Institute would recognize the special needs and the special relationship and would symbolize the special importance of our relations in the hemisphere; the president of the corporation would become a figure of major significance in hemisphere affairs.

d. Use of a corporation as the operating arm for the hemisphere would have the added advantage of assuring the continuity of programs under three-to-five-year contracts.

e. The present large staff which AID maintains in various countries would be reduced to a minimum; technicians would be sent to those countries only to carry out specific technical assistance programs or other agreed-upon assignments.

f. In addition, the Institute could provide assistance through contracts with private nonprofit organizations where desirable, thus multiplying the points of contact between all facets of our society and those of other hemisphere nations.

g. This corporation would have the power to set up subsidiaries to give special emphasis in fields of particular concern. Two such subsidiaries are specifically recommended:

—A Western Hemisphere Institute for Education, Science and Culture; and,

—An Inter-American Rural Development Corporation.

Each would be an operating corporation to carry out projects in its respective fields under the policy guidance of the President of the Institute of Western Hemisphere Affairs (further descriptions appear on pages 85, 115, and 124).

5. *We applaud the President's support of legislation now before Congress to create an* OVERSEAS PRIVATE INVESTMENT CORPORATION; *it should be enacted into law.*

a. OPIC would take over the activities relating to private economic development that are now being

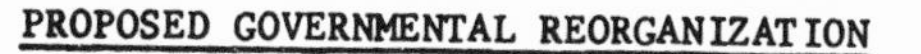
PROPOSED GOVERNMENTAL REORGANIZATION

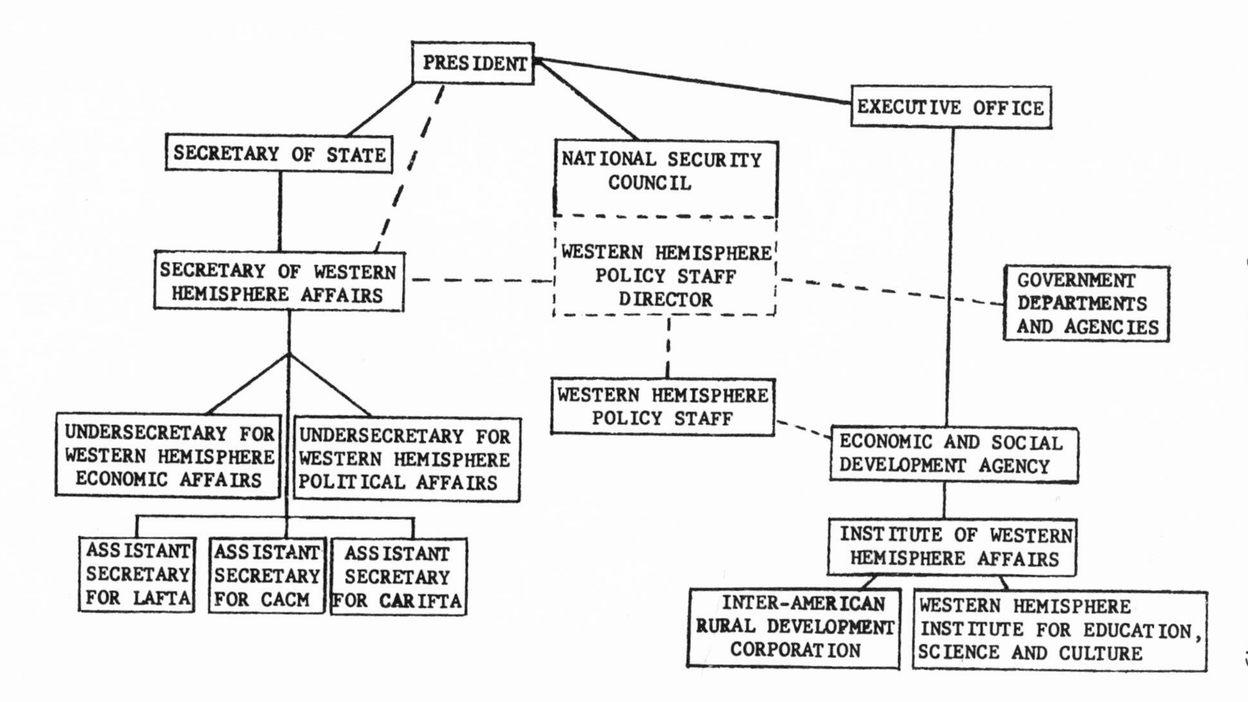
PRESIDENT
SECRETARY OF STATE
NATIONAL SECURITY COUNCIL
EXECUTIVE OFFICE
SECRETARY OF WESTERN HEMISPHERE AFFAIRS
WESTERN HEMISPHERE POLICY STAFF DIRECTOR
GOVERNMENT DEPARTMENTS AND AGENCIES
WESTERN HEMISPHERE POLICY STAFF
UNDERSECRETARY FOR WESTERN HEMISPHERE ECONOMIC AFFAIRS
UNDERSECRETARY FOR WESTERN HEMISPHERE POLITICAL AFFAIRS
ECONOMIC AND SOCIAL DEVELOPMENT AGENCY
INSTITUTE OF WESTERN HEMISPHERE AFFAIRS
ASSISTANT SECRETARY FOR LAFTA
ASSISTANT SECRETARY FOR CACM
ASSISTANT SECRETARY FOR CARIFTA
INTER-AMERICAN RURAL DEVELOPMENT CORPORATION
WESTERN HEMISPHERE INSTITUTE FOR EDUCATION, SCIENCE AND CULTURE

handled by AID, including insurance, contracts, loans, and investment surveys.

b. This would separate administration of government-to-government programs from private-enterprise activities—a desirable step since an agency operating primarily at a government-to-government level finds it difficult to get the orientation to handle private enterprise matters.

6. *The President should discuss with the leaders of the Senate and the House of Representatives the possibility of creating a* JOINT CONGRESSIONAL COMMITTEE *to coordinate legislative policy concerning the hemisphere.*

a. A broad-based steering committee could work with the appropriate committees of both houses of the Congress to anticipate hemisphere problems, consider new legislation, and review existing laws relating to hemisphere affairs.

b. This would be an important expression of congressional interest in a coordinated approach to the other hemisphere nations.

B. Country-by-Country Relations

The experiences of the mission in the course of its travels demonstrated anew that there is no substitute in the institutions and practices of diplomacy for the warmth and interplay of personal contact.

In country after country, members of the mission were told by our hosts of a feeling in that country that they had no real personal contact with the United States—that they were shut out by a wall of bureaucracy, the inability to get a decision, the low priorities for hemisphere matters, the fact there is no one with effective authority with whom they can talk.

It was apparent that the spirit of personal friendship and respect which characterized the "good neighbor" era had evaporated. It is vital to reestablish that spirit.

Each country in the hemisphere is unique, with its own special problems, its own special relations with other countries and with the United States. It is therefore vital that our diplomacy be geared to close and effective ties with each of these nations.

All nations in the hemisphere are interdependent in today's world. We must not lose sight of the need for close ties on a country-by-country basis—a purpose which the foregoing proposal for a Secretary of Western Hemisphere Affairs should greatly facilitate on behalf of the Secretary of State and the President.

RECOMMENDATION: NATIONAL POLICY OBJECTIVE

The United States should maintain close, open, intimate, and effective ties with each of the hemisphere nations, on a country-by-country basis, recognizing that each nation is different and that bilateral relations and programs have an important role to play.

C. Regional Organizations

As individual entities, many of the hemisphere countries have such limited resources that they could not promote economic growth and social progress or sustain an acceptable level of economic competition in world markets. Thus they have begun to form regional groupings to coordinate their economic policies.

The first of these regional groupings and the most effective thus far has been the Central American Common Market. It began with a limited list of "free trade" goods, was gradually broadened into fiscal agreements, and still later expanded to handle issues of economic and political significance.

An important instrument of the CACM is the Central American Bank for Economic Integration, which makes loans for public works, industry, agriculture, opening new markets, and other region-wide projects.

The Caribbean nations have a wide variety of regional organizations and are now forming a Caribbean Free Trade Association and a Caribbean Development Bank.

The treaty creating the Andean Group under the Latin American Free Trade Association was signed this summer. The River Plate countries have been discussing the possibility of a regional organization but have thus far made no commitment.

The Latin American Free Trade Association, which began in 1961 to reduce tariffs among eleven Latin American countries, is moving slowly because of the complexities of negotiating reciprocal tariff cuts among so many nations.

RECOMMENDATION: NATIONAL POLICY OBJECTIVE

The United States should cooperate with and support fully regional organizations among the nations of the Western Hemisphere.

RECOMMENDATIONS FOR ACTION

1. *Upon request, the United States should encourage regional organizations with financial and technical assistance and support for industrial, agricultural, educational, and scientific programs.*
2. *To facilitate such cooperation, the United States should appoint* ASSISTANT SECRETARIES OF WESTERN HEMISPHERE AFFAIRS *for the CACM nations, LAFTA, and the Caribbean nations.*
   —Since effective cooperation depends importantly on more frequent personal contacts, adequate air transport facilities for these Assistant Secretaries and leaders in the region would promote better understanding.

D. Inter-American Organizations

Necessary and important organizational changes have already been worked out to strengthen and revitalize the Organization of American States. Some of these require ratification by the individual governments—a process which is well advanced. However, there are some possible further initiatives which would extend its effectiveness.

During our travels, we heard varying viewpoints in regard to the Organization of American States. Some felt the United States dominated the organization. Others criticized it as ineffective in important fields. Yet the OAS is a constructive force in the hemisphere. It has dramatically demonstrated its merit anew in the political field with the successful negotiations to end the recent hostilities between El Salvador and Honduras. In the development area, the OAS is doing increasingly effective work. The reasons for this are: it minimizes political factors; it can impose and enforce more exacting project conditions and performance criteria; and it places greater responsibility in the hands of the countries themselves to manage available resources.

The Inter-American Committee for the Alliance for Progress (CIAP) of the OAS has done increasingly useful work in reviewing national development programs and projects.

In the area of security, the OAS can play an even more important role, but this will require increased authority and expanded structures—for the security structure of the OAS has not kept pace with the changing needs of the times.

The Inter-American Development Bank has made a major contribution, but technical rather than political consideration should be stressed in future loans. While the U.S. veto power over IDB loans has not been used, the threat of using the veto for political purposes has influenced decisions.

Recommendation: National Policy Objective

The United States should give full support to and work through the Organization of American States and its several Councils in dealing with Western Hemisphere affairs; it should reaffirm its adherence to the principles and policies set forth in the various treaties and conventions which form the general structure of the hemisphere.

Recommendations for Action

1. *Political: The United States should cooperate fully with the Organization of American States in dealing with the political problems of the hemisphere.*
2. *Economic and Social: The United States should make greater use of the multilateral channels of the OAS to execute technical assistance programs and should propose to the Inter-American Economic and Social Council that*

CIAP (the Council's executive arm) be assigned greater responsibility in planning, setting priorities for, and allocating development assistance for the nations of the Western Hemisphere, and that its name be changed to the WESTERN HEMISPHERE DEVELOPMENT COMMITTEE.

a. The United States in developing its assistance programs should work in close cooperation with the Western Hemisphere Development Committee and give full consideration to its recommendations for national and multi-national assistance programs and projects as provided in Title 6, Section 251 H, Foreign Assistance Act of 1966.

b. The United States should submit to an annual review by the Western Hemisphere Development Committee of its economic programs as originally agreed to in the Charter of Punta del Este.

3. *Education, Science, and Culture: When the Inter-American Council for Education, Scientific, and Cultural Affairs is ratified, the United States should undertake major programs to support its objectives.**

4. *Security: The United States through appropriate channels should propose a* WESTERN HEMISPHERE SECURITY COUNCIL *composed of civilian as distinct from military leaders with headquarters outside the United States.***

5. *Migration: The United States should stand ready to support the Organization of American States' initiatives toward facilitating desirable migrations within the hemisphere.*

—Working in cooperation with regional organizations, the OAS can make a major contribution toward negotiating and implementing migration from areas of overcrowding—as in El Salvador, for example—to countries seeking more people.

6. *CECLA: The United States should recognize the significance and the role of CECLA as an effective vehicle of independent expression for the other American nations.*

* See Recommendation, page 115.
** See Recommendation, page 63.

—The recommendations growing out of the recent Viña del Mar conference have been reviewed and considered in preparing this report. They have proved most helpful.

E. International Organizations

It is important that the special relationship which exists among nations in the Western Hemisphere not be misunderstood in the larger context of world-wide relationships.

Each nation in the hemisphere has its own role and contacts throughout the world. The quest for hemisphere unity and accelerated economic and social growth within the hemisphere should not be regarded as Western Hemisphere isolationism.

The United Nations and its specialized agencies should be fully supported and fully utilized by all the nations of the Western Hemisphere, together with the machinery and facilities of the "special relationship."

Recommendation: National Policy Objective

The United States should foster a world-wide outlook as complementary to rather than competitive with Western Hemisphere goals.

Recommendations for Action

1. *The United States should make use of international facilities, such as the World Bank and World Health Organization, in developing its regional assistance programs.*
2. *United States policy-makers should be ever mindful of the urgent need to avoid any tendency or even an appearance of a tendency toward isolationism inimical to the best interests of the hemisphere and the world at large.*

Chapter Four

POLICY AND ACTION

A. United States Political Relations with the Hemisphere

Throughout the hemisphere, there is growing uncertainty concerning the extent of the United States' commitment to work with the people of the other American republics for their economic and social betterment.

Our neighbors need to be reassured of our conviction that people are, indeed, our basic concern, and that we want to continue to work with them, regardless of the form of their government, to help them raise the level of their lives. In this way we can help strengthen the forces of democracy.

Commitment to representative, responsive democratic government is deeply imbedded in the collective political consciousness of the American people. We would like to see strong representative government develop in the other nations of the hemisphere for both idealistic and practical reasons:

—Our experience convinces us that representative democratic government and free societies offer the best means of organizing man's social, political, and economic life so as to maximize the prospects for improving the individual's dignity and the quality of his life.

—Practically, nations with broadly based political systems of a democratic type are more likely to have outlooks and concepts compatible with the style of the United States and its people, and more willing to cooperate with us in establishing an effective world order.

All Americans, in fact, share a common heritage of respect for human dignity, justice, and freedom of the individual. They are linked by the bonds of revolutionary ancestors who succeeded in declaring themselves separate from the nations of Europe. This heritage is evidenced in different ways in different nations, especially when they are at differing stages of development or reflect different cultural influences. Individualism in the American republics often takes a more intense form than it does in the United States, which has had a successful experience with greater individual restraints for the public benefit. It must be recognized that there is no single route to the fulfillment of human dignity.

Democracy is a very subtle and difficult problem for most of the other countries in the hemisphere. The authoritarian and hierarchical tradition which has conditioned and formed the cultures of most of these societies does not lend itself to the particular kind of popular government we are used to. Few of these countries, moreover, have achieved the sufficiently advanced economic and social systems required to support a consistently democratic system. For many of these societies, therefore, the question is less one of democracy or a lack of it than it is simply of orderly ways of getting along.

There will often be times when the United States will find itself in disagreement with the particular policies or forms of government of other American nations. However, the fundamental question for the United States is how it can cooperate to help meet the basic needs of the people of the hemisphere despite the philosophical disagreements it may have with the nature of particular regimes. It must seek pragmatic ways to help people without necessarily embracing their governments. It should recognize that diplomatic relations are merely practical conveniences and not measures of moral judgment. This can be done by maintaining formal lines of communication without embracing such regimes.

The U.S. should also recognize that political evolution takes time and that, realistically, its long-term interests will be served by maintaining at least minimal diplomatic relationships with other governments of the hemisphere while trying to find ways to assist the people of those countries, and to encourage the governments to move toward democratic processes. Such a policy requires a very difficult balance but is one that must be achieved pragmatically on a case-by-case basis. The U.S. cannot renege on its commitment to a better life for all of the people of the hemisphere because of moral disagreement with regimes which the people themselves did not establish and do not control.

RECOMMENDATION: NATIONAL POLICY OBJECTIVE

The United States should work with and for the people of this hemisphere to assist them in enhancing the quality of their lives and to provide moral leadership as a force for freedom and justice in the Americas.

The United States cannot allow disagreements with the form or the domestic policies of other American governments to jeopardize its basic objective of working with and for their people to our mutual benefit.

RECOMMENDATIONS FOR ACTION

The President should reaffirm our national commitment:

a. To work with and for the people of this hemisphere.
b. To recognize hemisphere governments in accordance with Article XXXV of the Act of the Ninth International Conference of American States in 1948—where it was stated: "The establishment or maintenance of diplomatic relations with a government does not imply any judgment upon the domestic policy of that government."
c. To the covenants* which bind together the nations of the Western Hemisphere in respect for the sovereignty of nations and opposition to foreign intervention.

In this connection, the President should endorse Senate Resolution 205 now pending before the Senate.

B. Western Hemisphere Security

If the quality of life for the individual in this hemisphere

* Fourth Conference of Buenos Aires (1910), establishing Pan American Union; Inter-American Treaty (1947); Charter of Organization of American States and conventions concluded at Bogotá Conference (1948), and current amendments to the charter; Charter for the Alliance for Progress (1961) and Declaration of the Presidents (1967).

is to be meaningful, there must be freedom from fear and full respect for the rights and the personal dignity of individuals —not just one's own rights and dignity, but everyone's.

Unfortunately, far too many people in the hemisphere—including people in the United States—are denied such freedom and respect. Forces of anarchy, terror, and subversion are loose in the Americas. Moreover, this fact has too long gone unheeded in the United States.

Doubt and cynicism have grown in the other American nations as to the purposefulness of the United States in facing this serious threat to freedom, democracy, and the vital interests of the entire hemisphere.

Many of our neighbors find it incomprehensible that the United States will not sell them military equipment which they feel is required to deal with internal subversion. They have been puzzled by the reduction in U.S. military assistance grants in view of the growing intensity of the subversive activities they face.

They were concerned that their young people were being drawn to Cuba in never-diminishing numbers, for indoctrination and for instruction in the arts of propaganda, the skills of subversion, and the tactics of terror.

Castro's recent restatement of his policy indicates no change in objectives. Rather, he reaffirms his revolutionary concepts and establishes a new set of priorities and conditions under which Cuban support for revolutionaries will be given.

The subversive capabilities of these communist forces are increasing throughout the hemisphere. The inflation, urban terrorism, racial strife, overcrowding, poverty, violence, and rural insurgency are all among the weapons available to the enemies of the systems of the free nations of the Western Hemisphere. These forces are quick to exploit for their own ends the freedoms afforded by democratic governments.

The seriousness of these factors when exploited by covert communist forces is not fully recognized in the United States.

Two decades and more ago, in the presence of an overt and world-wide Soviet threat, the United States response was realistic and flexible. It included in the Western Hemisphere the training and equipping of security forces for hemisphere defense.

Fortuitously, the military capability thus achieved subsequently enabled the individual nations of the hemisphere to deal with the initial impact of a growing, covert communist threat to their internal security. However, the threat has shifted from one based in the rural areas to one centered on urban terrorism. Realistic efforts to deal with this increasingly dangerous development are necessary on an effective, hemisphere-wide basis.

In addition, the United States must face more forthrightly the fact that while the military in the other American nations are alert to problems of internal security, they do not feel that this is their only role and responsibility. They are conscious of the more traditional role of a military establishment to defend the nation's territory, and they possess understandable professional pride which creates equally understandable desires for modern arms; in addition, they are subjected to the sales pressures and blandishments of suppliers from other nations—east and west—eager to sell. The result of all this is a natural resentment on the part of the military of other American nations when the United States refuses to sell modern items of equipment.

Thus many military leaders in the other American republics see the United States acting to hold them back as second-class citizens, and they are becoming increasingly estranged from us at a time when their political role is on the rise. Our dilemma is how to be responsive to their legitimate desires for modern equipment without encouraging the diversion of scarce resources from development to armaments which, in some cases, may be unrelated to any real security requirement.

Military leaders throughout the hemisphere are frequently criticized here in the United States. However, we will have to give increasing recognition to the fact that many new military leaders are deeply motivated by the need for social and economic progress. They are searching for ways to bring education and better standards of living to their people while avoiding anarchy or violent revolution. In many cases, it will be more useful for the United States to try to work with them in these efforts, rather than to abandon or insult them because we are conditioned by arbitrary ideological stereotypes.

In addition, there is not in the United States a full appreciation of the important role played by the police. There is a tendency in the United States to equate the police in the other American republics with political action and repression, rather than with security. There have, unfortunately, been many such instances of the use of police. Yet well-motivated, well-trained police, when present in local communities, enforce the laws, protect the citizenry from terror, and discourage criminal elements. At the present time, however, police forces of many countries have not been strengthened as population and great urban growth have taken place. Consequently they have become increasingly less capable of providing either the essential psychological support or the internal security that is their major function.

Moreover, the people of the United States do not recognize that, as a whole, the other American nations spend a smaller percentage of their Gross National Product on defense than any other area except Africa south of the Sahara. Most of this expenditure, despite much talk of supersonic aircraft, is for personnel and operating costs. Relatively little has been spent on major items of equipment. For this reason, most of the military inventories of these other hemisphere nations consist of equipment acquired shortly after World War II. Such equipment is becoming obsolete and unserviceable, and spare parts are becoming increasingly unavailable.

One other point not clearly understood in the United States is that no one country today can effectively protect its own internal security by itself.

The youth that go abroad for training in subversive activities, the money and directives that flow through agents, and the propaganda that comes from outside their borders are all beyond their effective control.

Only through hemisphere cooperation can these problems, which so vitally affect internal security, be adequately dealt with.

RECOMMENDATION: NATIONAL POLICY OBJECTIVE

The United States should cooperate with other nations of the Western Hemisphere in measures to strengthen internal security.

RECOMMENDATIONS FOR ACTION

1. *A Western Hemisphere Security Council*
   a. The United States should work with the other republics to form a civilian-directed Western Hemisphere Security Council to cope with the forces of subversion that operate throughout the Western Hemisphere. The purpose of the Council would be to help the hemisphere countries work together in creating and preserving the kind of orderly environment, free from terror and violence, in which each citizen of each country can build a better life for himself and his family. This Council would supersede the Special Consultative Committee on Security of the Organization of American States.
   b. Although the United States would have membership in the Council, the Council should have its headquarters outside of our country.
2. *A Western Hemisphere Security Training Assistance Program*
   a. The United States should reverse the recent downward trend in grants for assisting the training of security forces for the other hemisphere countries. (The total amount proposed for fiscal year 1970 is $21.4 million, as against $80.7 million in fiscal year 1966.) In view of the growing subversion against hemisphere government, the mounting terrorism and violence against citizens, and the rapidly expanding population, it is essential that the training program which brings military and police personnel from the other hemisphere nations to the United States and to training centers in Panama be continued and strengthened.
   b. The name "Military Assistance Program" should be dropped because it no longer reflects the security emphasis we believe important. The program should be renamed the "Western Hemisphere Security Program."
3. *Internal Security Support*
   a. The United States should respond to requests for assistance of the police and security forces of the

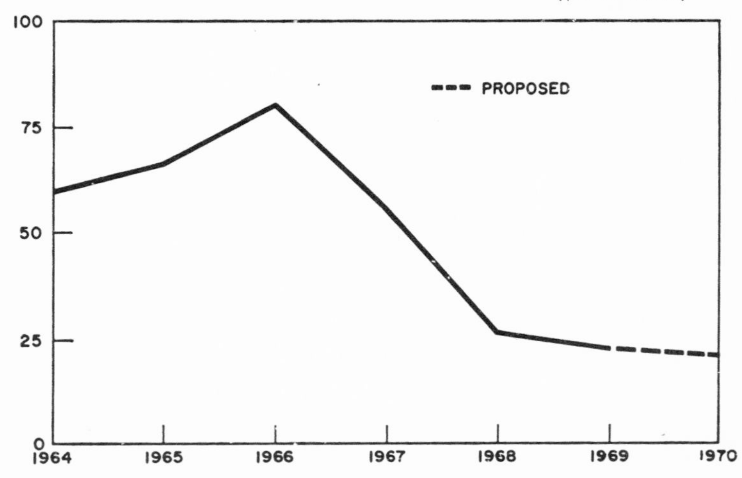

hemisphere nations by providing them with the essential tools to do their job.

b. Accordingly, the United States should meet reasonable requests from other hemisphere governments for trucks, jeeps, helicopters, and like equipment to provide mobility and logistical support for these forces; for radios, and other command control equipment for proper communications among the forces; and for small arms for security forces.

c. In furtherance of these objectives, the United States should provide, on request, military and technical training missions but should no longer maintain the permanent military missions in residence in other nations which too often have constituted too large and too visible a United States presence.

4. *Military Sales for Defense*

a. The Executive Branch should seek modification of the Conte and Symington amendments to permit the United States to sell aircraft, ships, and other major military equipment without aid-cut penalties to the more developed nations of the hemisphere when these nations believe this equipment is necessary to protect their land, patrol their seacoasts and airspace, and otherwise maintain the morale of their forces and protect their sovereignty. Realistically, if the United States doesn't sell such equipment, it will be purchased from other sources, east or west, and this would not be compatible with the United States' best interests.

b. Each country should be permitted to buy such equipment through purchase orders placed with the United States Defense Department through the Military Assistance Program, in order that each country may get full value for its military investment, more reliable delivery dates, and better maintenance.

C. Economic and Social Development

Our common objective—to improve the quality of life for all individuals in the hemisphere—can only be accomplished by working together to accelerate the rate of economic and social development. Hemisphere interdependence in these matters is more than a theory. It is a fact of life.

The Alliance for Progress was the first formal agreement among Western Hemisphere nations on specific goals related to economic and social development. The goals of the Alliance remain the best expression of our common objectives. To be sure, actual progress under the Alliance has not come up to the grand hopes entertained in 1961 at Punta del Este. Yet the broad Alliance objectives of economic and social development to enrich the lives of individuals remain the challenging goals which Western Hemisphere nations seek.

One of the least understood features of the Alliance is the fact that it is a self-help effort in which the principal responsibility for financing and implementation has been with the people of the other hemisphere countries. It is not a bilateral United States aid program, contrary to popular impression. The United States is but one partner in a development effort which is about 90 per cent financed by the other American republics.*

* CIAP Document: Meeting 17 March 1969.

To say the Alliance has failed is to discount the genuine progress it has made. The fact is that many of the expectations generated at the outset of the Alliance were unrealistic. But the Alliance experience shows that man *can* shape the future along lines which will contribute to broad national and hemispheric objectives, and this is the important fact. To be sure, mistakes are made, but progress frequently involves the process of learning through mistakes.

One of the things learned from the mission was that other nations have deeply resented the way in which the United States has carried out its assistance programs. As part of the aid effort, the United States has intervened, usually with the best of intentions, in almost every aspect of their economic policies and programs. It has too often tried to do things *for* them, because it felt it could do them better. This subconscious paternalism was less effective not only because it was resented, but also because it did not give the other nations an incentive to assume responsibility and initiative themselves.

It is clear that most of the American republics are psychologically ready to assume direction of their own development efforts. Moreover, the technical capabilities of the individual nations and the international lending institutions are growing steadily. The time has arrived for the United States to move consciously from a paternalistic role to one of partnership. The United States must build on the progress already achieved, and improve and accelerate its efforts, but it also must be willing to help without trying to dominate. Shifting an increasing portion of our assistance through multilateral institutions would help to accomplish this objective.

The other American nations must assume greater responsibility for their own performance in utilizing United States resources. They also must recognize that their performance will influence the extent to which the United States Congress and public will be willing to maintain or increase levels of cooperation with the Western Hemisphere.

The challenge now is to develop pragmatic programs which build on the long experience of hemisphere cooperation and which will accelerate economic and social progress.

The procedure involves:

1. Efforts to improve policies and programs which have produced generally constructive results;

2. A resolve to modify or drop those which have not stood the test of time; and,

3. Most importantly, a willingness throughout the hemisphere to innovate by developing new policies and programs to meet common objectives.

Economic and social development must go hand-in-hand. Economic growth provides the wherewithal to support improved diets, health and sanitation, enhanced educational opportunities, better housing, and all the elements which contribute to an improvement in the quality of life. The process, however, is not automatic. Positive policies and actions are

LATIN AMERICA
AVERAGE ANNUAL GROWTH OF GNP

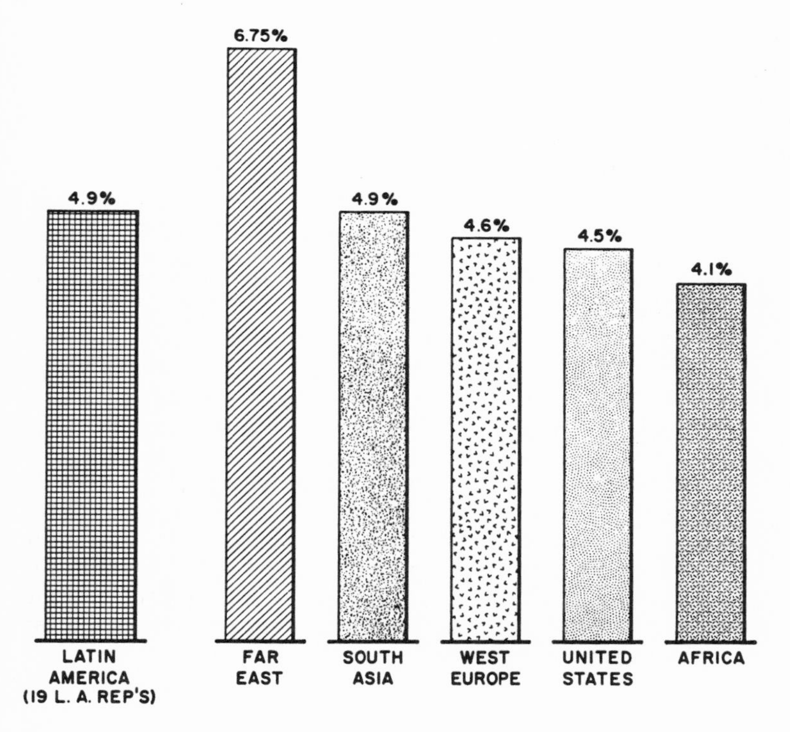

Source: A.I.D.

called for to make sure that the benefits of economic growth are used effectively to provide expanding horizons of opportunity for all individuals. Thus social development is not only made possible by economic growth but is essential to make sure the benefits of growth are broadly shared.

ECONOMIC PROGRESS

The rate of overall economic progress in the rest of the Western Hemisphere outside of Canada and the United States compares favorably with other regions of the world so far in the 1960's. Gross National Product in constant prices has advanced at an average annual rate of 4.9 per cent.

But in terms of improving the quality of life for individuals, progress has not been satisfactory. The rate of population growth in other Western Hemisphere nations—2.9 per cent per annum—is the highest of any major area in the world. Thus, the 4.9 per cent annual increase in total production has yielded an increase of 2 per cent per annum in production per person. This measure is more meaningful, since it is production per person which supports the rise in living standards for individuals.

If these trends are projected, they show that overall Gross National Product would double in fifteen years—while it would take thirty-five years to double the per capita production which supports the rise in living standards for individuals.

This is just not good enough.

One way out lies in increasing the rate of growth in Gross National Product, and this should be a broad hemisphere objective. Yet long experience shows that it is extremely difficult to achieve and maintain overall economic growth rates of 5 to 6 per cent or more. Simple arithmetic shows that, even with a maximum effort to step up the pace of economic growth, there are only limited possibilities of producing the desired rise in living standards for such a rapidly growing population.

However, experience supports the view that, in time, the general social and cultural changes that are a part of broad development may operate to slow the rate of population growth. Such processes work slowly, however. Thus the problem must be faced now.

The rate of population growth in many of the nations of

the Western Hemisphere is so high that it will prove extremely difficult, if not impossible, to meet the economic and social objectives of steady, meaningful improvement in the life of individuals. This problem must be faced realistically.

There is widespread agreement that the most important elements in economic development are investment, technology, management, and markets (including those abroad). Govern-

GROWTH OF GNP AND PER CAPITA PRODUCTION

GNP YEARLY INCREASE OF 4.9%
DOUBLES IN 15 YEARS

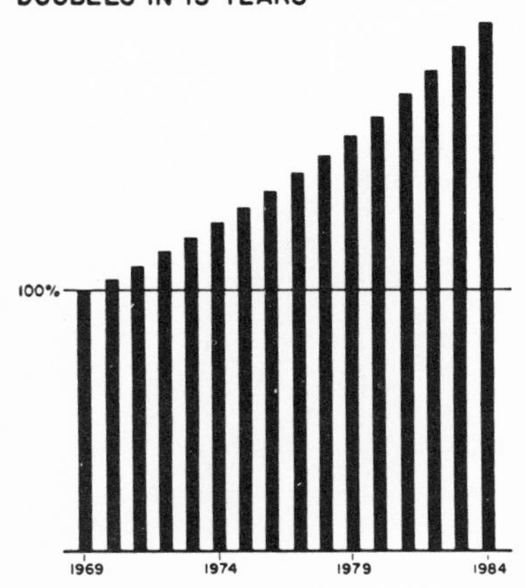

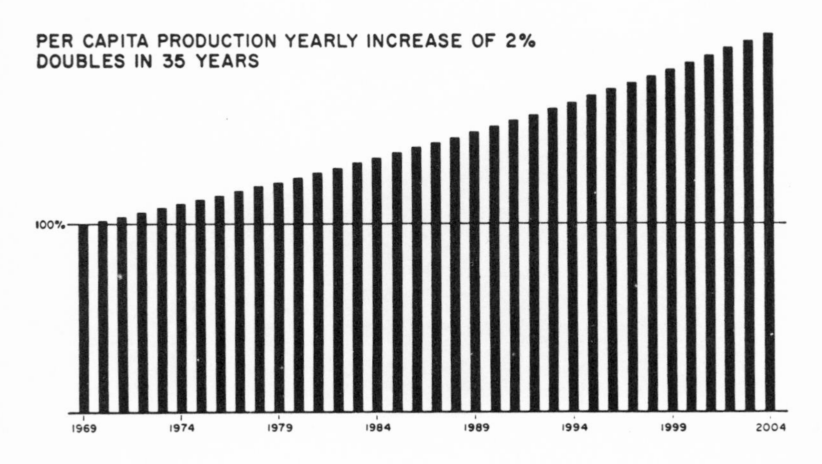

ment policies can encourage or deter development to the extent they contribute to these key elements by supporting education, encouraging savings, providing a favorable climate for domestic and foreign investment, and developing the necessary infrastructure.

While it is true that the main impetus for development must come from within nations, it is also true that hemisphere cooperation must provide the support which is essential for accelerated progress. Trade policies on the part of industrial nations can have a major influence on opportunities for export expansion on the part of the developing nations. Development assistance by the United States and the governments of other industrial nations can provide loans, grants, and technical assistance to supplement local efforts, primarily in such fields as public works, education, agriculture, and health. Foreign private investment can provide essential technical knowledge and capital.

1. TRADE POLICIES

Trade policy is the central economic issue facing all Western Hemisphere nations. Freer access to markets in the United

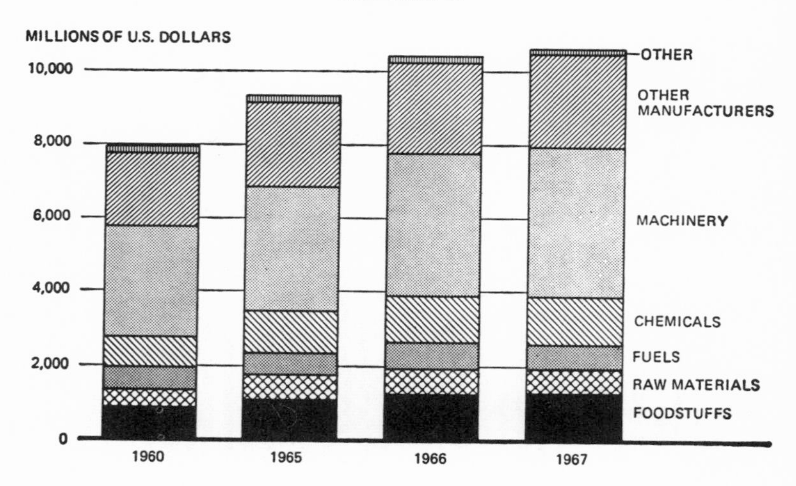

States and other industrial countries is essential to support accelerated economic progress. Provision of such opportunities poses problems of adjustment for the industrial nations in terms of jobs and investment. The challenge is to work together to develop a practical approach which will be in the best interests of all hemisphere nations.

Expanding export trade is the soundest and most important way the other American republics can finance the imports needed for broad development. In 1967 their export earnings were six times the net inflow of private and public capital from abroad. The great bulk of the area's $10.3 billion of imports consisted of the machinery and equipment needed to support industrialization and to expand governmental services, i.e., power, highways, and communications.

The slow growth in exports in the 1960's has been an important factor limiting the pace of general development. From 1960 to 1968 the value of the area's exports increased 4.7

PERCENTAGE INCREASE IN WORLD & LATIN AMERICA EXPORTS

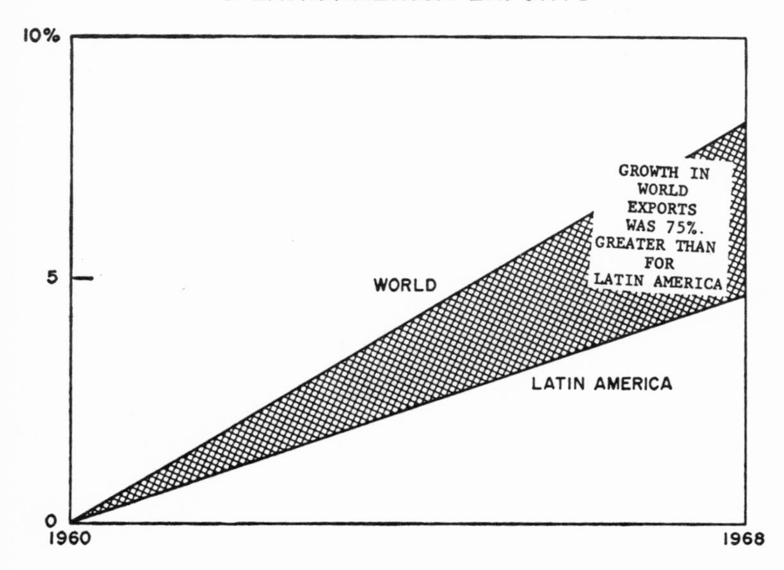

Source: International Monetary Fund

per cent per annum as compared with an increase of 8.2 per cent for world exports. Growth in world exports was 75 per cent greater than that for other hemisphere nations.

Exports By Commodity

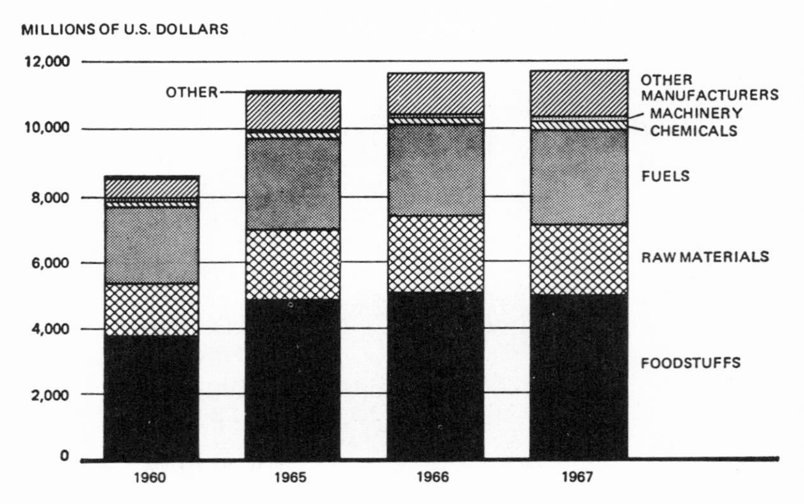

Source: ECLA. 13th Session, Lima, Peru

A major problem is that 87 per cent of the area's exports consists of primary products—food, natural fibers, and industrial raw materials. In contrast, almost two-thirds of the exports of the industrial nations are made up of manufactured products.

While sound policy calls for a maximum effort to diversify and develop exports of primary products at stable prices, it is unlikely that such exports can expand rapidly enough to support accelerated growth in the area as a whole. Though some nations have favorable opportunities in such fields, most of the countries must look to industrialization and increasing exports of industrial products.

Industrial development requires broad markets for efficient production. Domestic markets in most of the nations of the hemisphere are too limited for broad industrialization. Regional trading arrangements offer one constructive way to broaden markets. But even with a rapid development of regional markets, freer access to markets in industrial nations will be needed to support the industrial growth required to improve the quality of life through the hemisphere.

In the face of this imperative need for expanding trade, the United States imposes formidable barriers against imports from other Western Hemisphere nations:

—Imports of many primary products are subject to quotas.

—United States tariffs are so high on processed raw materials* and on the manufactured goods the area could export to the United States that they are serious impediments to trade.

It comes down to the elemental fact that trade expansion is essential to support accelerated economic development in the hemisphere. In the process, individuals throughout the hemisphere can benefit. There will be adjustment problems which must be dealt with in realistic terms. But a broader division of labor on a hemisphere basis can bring lower prices to consumers, higher wages for workers, and satisfactory incentives for saving and investment.

Increasing imports by the United States from other hemisphere nations will help expand United States exports to them. Last year, the United States imported goods valued at $4.3 billion from the area and exported $4.7 billion to these countries, for a favorable trade balance of over $400 million. United States exports to other hemisphere nations have grown 41 per cent since 1962, as against an increase of 59 per cent in the United States exports to the rest of the world.

The problem is not that the United States has lost competitive position—its share of exports to Latin America from all industrial nations has been quite stable in recent years. The fact is that the slow growth in the export earnings of the other countries in the hemisphere restricts their ability to finance imports. The record shows clearly that if the United States buys more from these countries, they will spend more on United States exports.

* For example, the producer of a raw material, which could be beans for soluble coffee, might ship the raw material duty free and get $1 a pound. If he processes the beans and ships soluble coffee, he might get $1.50 a pound and pay a 20 per cent tariff—not on the added value but on the full price. Thus the protection to the United States producer would not be 20 per cent, but 30¢ of the 50¢ added value, or an effective rate of 60 per cent.

UNITED STATES EXPORTS TO WORLD
($US millions)

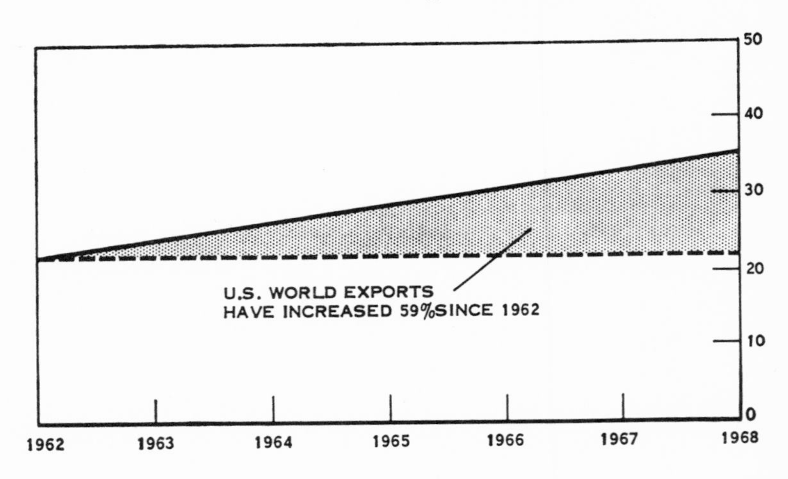

U.S. EXPORTS TO LATIN AMERICA

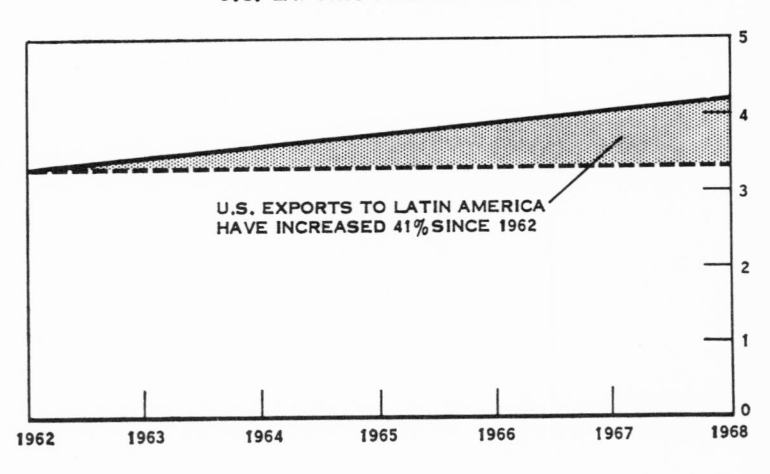

SOURCE – U.S. DEPT. OF COMMERCE

Recommendation: National Policy Objective

The United States should press for the maximum feasible development of mutually beneficial trade with other nations of the hemisphere. A doubling of such trade by 1976 is a realistic goal. This can only be accomplished by United States action to revise its tariffs and quotas to promote such mutually beneficial increased trade.

Recommendations for Action

1. *The United States should work out a balanced approach to the problem of expanding hemisphere trade in industrial products by moving to a system of tariff preferences for imports from all developing nations.*
   a. Tariff preferences should be phased in to avoid sudden large impacts and to provide time to make necessary adjustments.
   b. The United States should make vigorous efforts to secure agreement on the part of other industrial nations to extend generalized preferences to all developing nations. Until such agreement is reached, the United States would extend preferences only to nations which are not receiving special treatment from other industrial countries.
   c. Tariff preferences should be extended to those items where careful study shows the benefits to United States consumers clearly outweigh the costs of the adjustment.
   d. In return for tariff preferences, the developing nations should agree to a gradual reduction in their barriers to imports from the industrial nations—over a time period which might be as long as ten to twenty years. In this way, their infant industries can grow to a stature in which they are fully competitive in world markets.
   e. The United States should press through GATT for strict adherence to the rules of fair competition in international trade. It should act positively to apply countervailing duties where there is a clear pre-

sumption that other nations are violating the rules with subsidies, under whatever guise.

2. *Realistic and effective arrangements should be set up to assist United States workers and producers who are adversely affected by increased imports.*
   a. It is extremely important that new procedures be devised and supporting funds be provided to make sure that adjustment assistance is provided to workers and employers when there is a prima facie case of displacement because of increased imports.
   b. An adjustment program was part of the Kennedy round of tariff negotiations of 1967, but it was never effective because the conditions were too strict.
3. *Where the United States applies import quotas for domestic reasons, as in meat and cotton textiles, the allotments to hemisphere nations should be readjusted to assure that they*

PRICES OF DOMESTIC BEEF AND IMPORTED COOKED AND CANNED BEEF

NOTE: This table illustrates that imported cooked and canned beef are clearly low priced in relation to domestic lean cuts and beef manufacturing material. This class of beef items is, in turn, favorably priced against quality beef. Permitting imports to supplement domestic supplies can help to hold down the cost of living for low-income families.

	Twelve Months Ending June 30, 1968
Domestic:	
Fresh Boneless Chucks	$0.875 *
Fresh Beef Ham Insides	1.14 *
Imported:	
Prepared or Preserved Beef from Argentina	0.575 **
Canned Beef from Argentina	0.385 **
Canned Beef from Paraguay	0.40 **

SOURCE: Madigan, Abraham & Associates, Inc., "Imported Cooked Beef —Place in U.S. Beef Economy," Sarasota, Florida; June 6, 1969, p. 46.

* Prices calculated on the basis of a 40 per cent shrink to be comparable with cooked beef.
** Average landed value.

contribute to the general objectives of hemisphere development.

—As a general principle, the United States should allocate a major part of the growth in its imports to hemisphere nations. Changes in the allocation of quotas, even though relatively small in relation to United States consumption, can be of great benefit to some hemisphere nations.

4. *The United States should support commodity agreements which operate to stabilize and maintain prices for primary products at levels that reflect fair wages and other costs of production.*
   a. Where possible, such agreements should provide funds and mechanisms to control surplus production by offering incentives to diversification and increased efficiency.
   b. Price targets under such agreements should not be set so high as to provide incentives for the development of synthetic products which will replace natural products. With the tremendous advances in technology, this is a serious consideration.
   c. It should be recognized that under such agreements United States consumers are providing a form of necessary assistance to producing nations. The producing countries on their part should ensure that benefits are broadly shared in a manner which supports general development.
5. *The United States should use its voting power in the International Coffee Agreement, together with other Western Hemisphere nations, to make sure that the system works as effectively as possible in terms of its objectives relating to prices and quotas, and that Western Hemisphere nations receive a major share in the growth of the United States market.*
   a. It has been estimated that a drop of 1¢ per pound in the price of coffee means a loss of $55 million in foreign exchange to the fourteen coffee-producing countries of the Western Hemisphere.
   b. The United States should urge reconsideration of and support the measures advanced at the last meeting of the executive board of the International Coffee

Movement of Wholesale Prices of Quality and Economy Beef (Domestic and Imported) 1950-1968

The Increase in the Price of Economy Beef Comparable To that of Choice is likely to continue as the result of Restrictions on imported Supplies

(CARLOT sales, cents per Lb., Chicago basis)

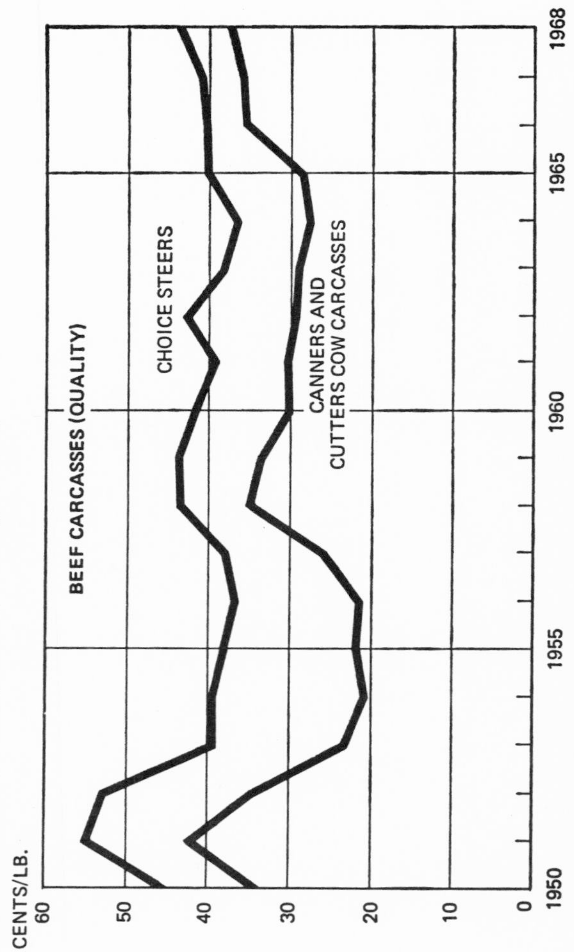

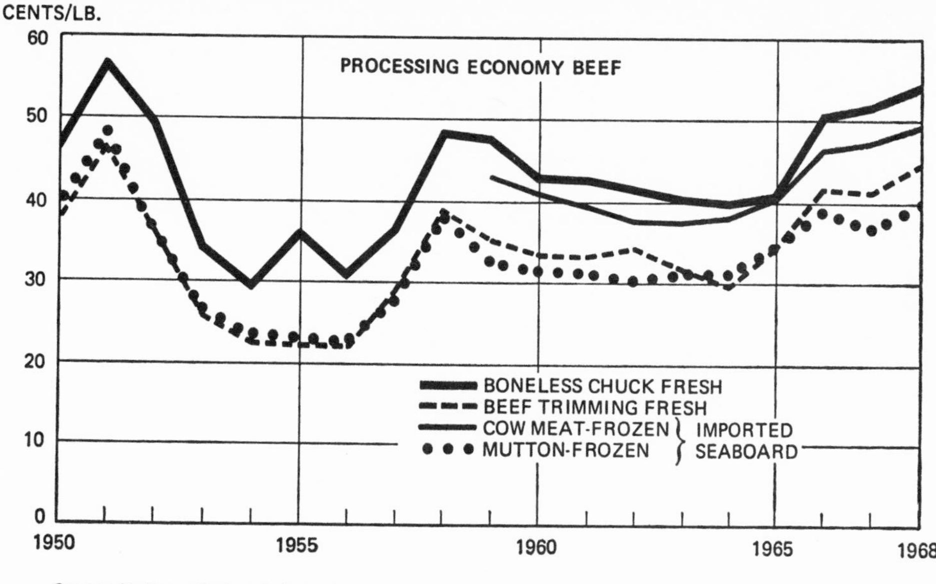

Source: Madigan, Abraham & Assoc., Inc.
"Imported Cooked Beef – Place in U.S. Economy"
Sarasota, Florida, 1969

Note: The above indicates the different movement of wholesale prices of quality and economy beef, the latter class including imports as well. Prices of economy cuts, reflecting the combined failure of domestic production and restricted imports to provide sufficient increases in per capita supplies. Prior to 1966, the entire class of economy beef was much cheaper in relation to quality beef than it has been since then. Further restriction of imported supplies would certainly result in continued price increases. Hardest hit, of course, are low income families, who now find that economy beef costs as much as choice cuts.

Council to correct the weaknesses that are preventing the coffee agreement from fully achieving its basic objectives.

6. *Special attention should be directed to the requirements of the Western Hemisphere nations when sugar quotas are reviewed in 1971.*
   a. A larger share of the growth in the United States market should be assigned to other hemisphere nations.
   b. A major problem concerns the adjustments which would be required if and when trading relations are resumed between the members of the Organization of American States and Cuba. A program should be set up for advance planning and consultation with sugar-producing nations in the hemisphere so that such a contingency could be handled through a phasing-in of Cuban sugar imports with minimum disruption of the market.
7. *The United States should lend its support to regional markets as they develop in the area, including participation in regional development banks.*
8. *The rates set by shipping conferences on United States trade with other hemisphere nations should be reviewed.*
   —In many cases, it costs two to three times as much to ship from a United States port as it does from Europe. This imposes a serious competitive disadvantage on United States exporters.

2. DEVELOPMENT ASSISTANCE

United States assistance has played a helpful role in hemisphere development, not so much in terms of the amount of aid—which can only be marginal to a country's own resources —but by placing assistance at the right place at the right time. It has, for example, financed the needed education or health projects which could not be funded elsewhere, or made possible a child-feeding program, or supported comprehensive land reform. More significantly, in some cases, United States assistance appears to have supplied the margin of resources that permitted a country to break out of stagnation and bring rampant inflation under control, thus helping millions of people.

In this way the $1 billion a year which represents the United States commitment to the Alliance for Progress has made its contribution. In the process, a number of lessons have been learned:

(1) Assistance can be fully effective only where a country is making maximum use of its own productive resources.

(2) In some cases, additional assistance from the United States and elsewhere can help a country move into a phase of self-sustaining growth, where ultimately foreign assistance is no longer needed.

(3) Distributing United States assistance in small and inadequate amounts to a country, where it makes little impact on development, can be a misuse and waste of funds.

(4) Multi-national and regional lending institutions have made great strides in filling the needs of developing nations for project loans. These organizations have the advantages of drawing on the skills and resources of many countries rather than one, and of being better able to avoid the political frictions that can develop in bilateral programs.

Impediments to Aid Program

In addition, certain problems have arisen which reduce the effectiveness of the assistance program:

(1) The United States assistance program has become increasingly encumbered with conditions and restrictions which seriously reduce the effectiveness of our assistance. These include requirements to ship half the goods purchased with assistance loans on United States freighters; provision that all imports be purchased in the United States no matter how much more expensive; earmarking of funds contrary to the particular needs of a country; and threats to withhold aid if United States investments are expropriated without appropriate payment, if a nation purchases "sophisticated" weapons, or if United States commercial fishing boats are taken into custody and fined.

(2) These encumbrances, when viewed separately, may appear reasonable—and, of course, they are to the advantage of special-interest groups in the United States. Taken together, however, they seriously weaken our efforts to assist developing countries. Some of them appear to violate the sovereignty of other nations. They also increase costs by requiring, for example, that imports for a construction project come from the

U.S. GOVERNMENT NET FOREIGN ASSISTANCE IN 1967

PERCENT SHARE

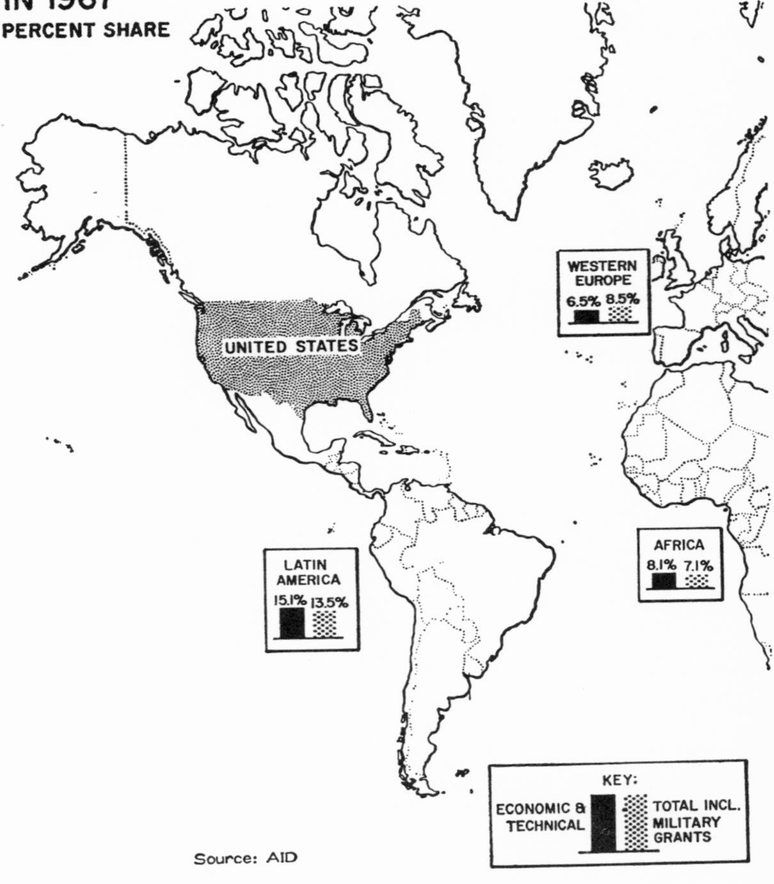

UNITED STATES

WESTERN EUROPE
6.5% 8.5%

AFRICA
8.1% 7.1%

LATIN AMERICA
15.1% 13.5%

KEY:
ECONOMIC & TECHNICAL
TOTAL INCL. MILITARY GRANTS

Source: AID

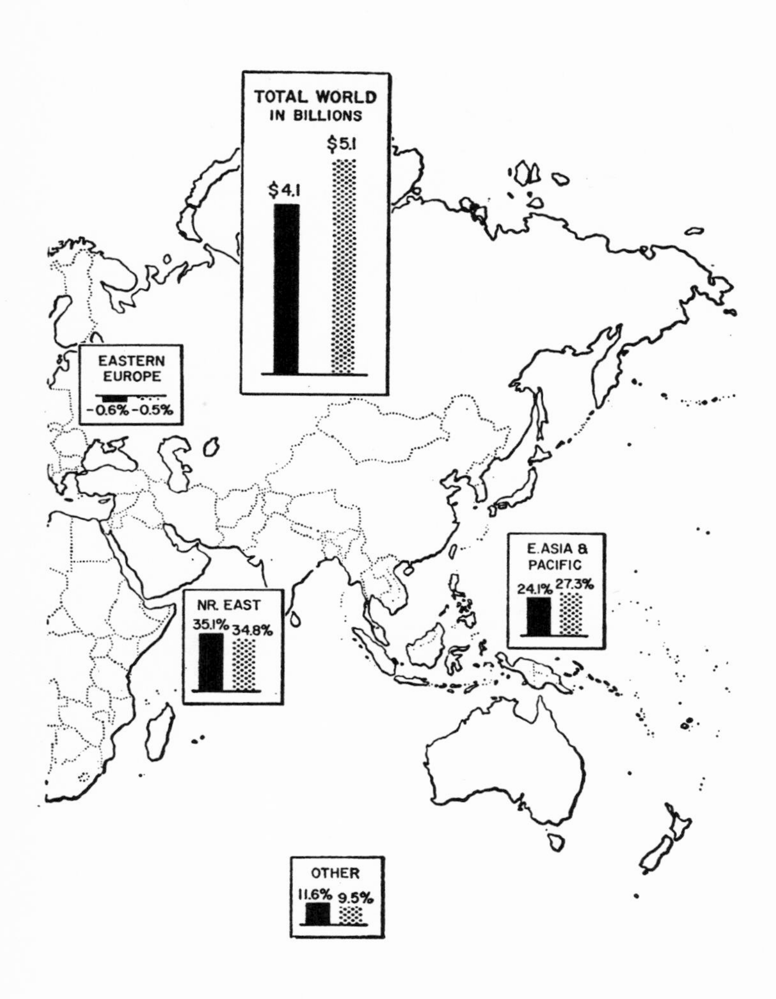
TOTAL WORLD
IN BILLIONS
$4.1
$5.1
EASTERN
EUROPE
-0.6% -0.5%
NR. EAST
35.1% 34.8%
E. ASIA &
PACIFIC
24.1% 27.3%
OTHER
11.6% 9.5%

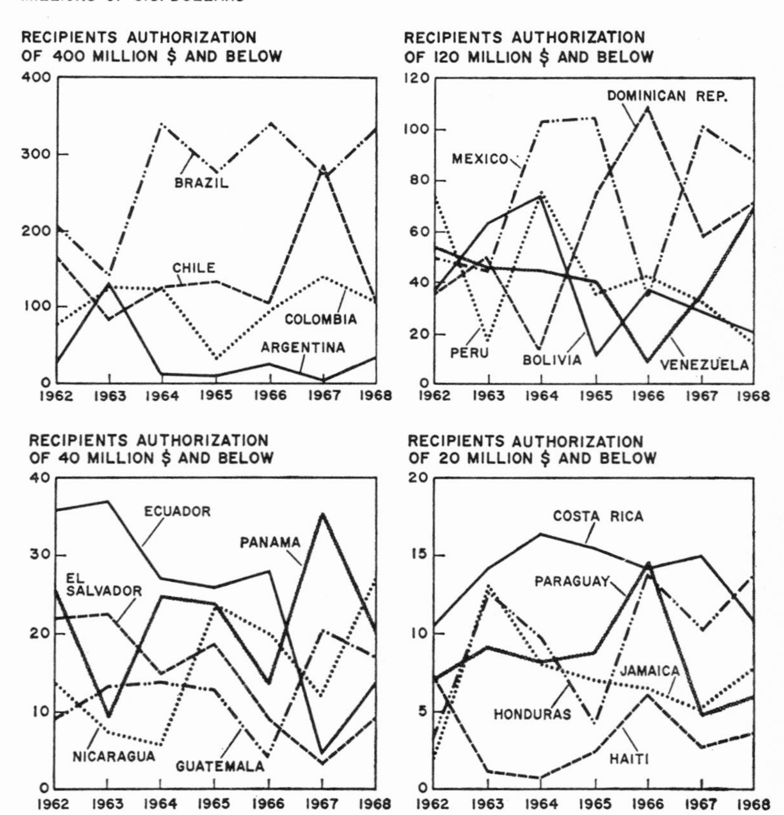

Source: US Overseas Loans & Grants

United States and that United States engineering firms be employed regardless of cost.

To be sure, United States government funds must be expended under the most careful controls. Existing controls are exacting in preventing waste and misuse of assistance funds from the United States point of view. But from the point of view of the recipient country, loading extraneous conditions on development loans amounts to waste and misuse of funds which they must repay with interest.

Recommendation: National Policy Objective

The United States should make a renewed policy commitment to support development in the Western Hemisphere as a means of improving the quality of life for individuals. Assistance should be provided without special-interest considerations and with due attention to self-help and country performance.

Recommendations for Action

1. *Development or program loans should be made on a three-to-five-year commitment basis, through the proposed Institute of Western Hemisphere Affairs,* which should become our most important assistance technique.*

    a. Such loans are designed to finance the overall development of a country, rather than any one specific project such as a power plant or a road. The loan provides dollars to finance imports. Importers pay for such items in local currency which can be used by the local governments for farm credit, urban development, and comparable purposes.

    b. The dollar loans are made to local governments on the basis of performance in terms of broad development goals, such as increasing exports, curbing inflation, or improving agriculture. Such loans would be made only to countries which have competent

*The economic operating arm for the Western Hemisphere of the proposed Economic and Social Development Agency (see page 47).

planning organizations and effective governmental administrative agencies.

2. *Multi-national and regional lending institutions should finance the bulk of public works projects and project loans should be restricted to agriculture, education, public health, and urban development projects which involve pioneering and testing new approaches.*
3. *In providing both program and project assistance, the United States should take full cognizance of the recommendations of the proposed Western Hemisphere Development Committee of the Organization of American States, giving full weight to Title 6, Section 251 H of the Foreign Assistance Act of 1966.*
4. *Development assistance loans should carry low interest rates and lenient repayment terms in order to be effective.*
    a. The basic concern of the United States lies not in how much interest is paid, but whether the funds "pay off" in helping a country develop.
    b. What the Marshall Plan accomplished almost entirely with grants of aid cannot be accomplished today in the developing countries with loans at high rates of interest.
5. *The encumbrances on United States assistance programs should be removed in all cases where they interfere with the process of development or impugn the sovereignty of other countries.*

    —An important start has been made by the present Administration in substantially modifying the "additionality" clause by greatly expanding the list of items that must be purchased. Actually, the concept of "additionality" should be eliminated entirely.
6. *Loan restrictions should be eased so borrowers can spend the funds anywhere in the Western Hemisphere with due consideration to questions of quality, price, and delivery dates.*

    —Local contractors and technicians should be used wherever possible with United States advisers where necessary.
7. *The Executive Branch should seek the suspension or modifications of the Pelley, Conte, Hickenlooper, Symington, and Roess amendments which affect the extension of*

assistance including cutoffs where countries purchase sophisticated weapons, or seize United States fishing boats operating without a license, or expropriate without due compensation.

8. *The provision that half of the goods financed by the United States must go in United States freighters should be repealed.*

It has been estimated that this provision reduces the effectiveness of each $1.00 of United States assistance by as much as 20¢. It is one of the major irritants felt in developing countries. This is a disguised subsidy to United States shipping companies. Any necessary subsidy should be given openly and directly by congressional appropriation.

3. Debt Service Problems

In the effort to support accelerated economic development, the major financial mechanism used has been loans from multinational and regional agencies, governments, and private sources. Many of the loans from multi-national and regional institutions and from governments are "soft" loans in the sense that interest rates are low and terms of repayment are lenient. The concept of soft loans is basically sound—they provide real assistance, while the fact that they must be repaid helps keep the development process realistic.

Nevertheless, interest and amortization payments must be made on schedule on all loans, from public and private sources, if a country is to maintain its credit standing. Heavy borrowings by some Western Hemisphere countries to support development have reached the point where annual repayments of interest and amortization absorb a large share of foreign exchange earnings. Within five years a number of other nations in the Western Hemisphere could face the same situation. Many of the countries are, in effect, having to make new loans to get the foreign exchange to pay interest and amortization on old loans, and at higher interest rates.

This debt service problem is a major concern. If countries get into a position where interest and amortization payments on foreign loans require a disproportionately large share of available foreign exchange, then the general pace of development will be slowed by the inability to maintain imports of the capital equipment needed to support economic growth.

RECOMMENDATION: NATIONAL POLICY OBJECTIVE

The United States policy for the Western Hemisphere should recognize the multiple advantages of a GENEROUS RESCHEDULING OF DEBT SERVICE REQUIREMENTS *for countries facing balance of payment problems.*

RECOMMENDATIONS FOR ACTION

1. *Studies of the debt service problem on a country-by-country basis should be initiated by the Western Hemisphere Development Committee (the present CIAP).*
   a. In this way, problems can be anticipated and dealt with in advance through an appropriate rescheduling by the United States Government of the dollar payments of interest and amortization.
   b. In addition, CIAP should be encouraged to discuss with the Inter-American Development Bank and other international lending institutions the possibility of stretching out loan payments for countries that have debt problems.
2. *Where dollar payments are suspended or stretched out, the equivalent amounts in local currencies should be paid into a special fund to be used—in consultation with the United States—to meet the general development objectives of the other Western Hemisphere nations. These would include:*
   a. Financing exports of capital goods within the region;
   b. Financing expanded economic development through national and regional development banks; and
   c. Financing local private participation in local joint ventures with foreign capital.

4. PRIVATE SAVINGS AND INVESTMENT

Accelerated economic growth will require increasing flows of private investment, local and foreign. Yet in all too many cases, private savings and investment are held back by high and erratic rates of inflation as well as by complex government controls and restrictions. Moreover, too large a portion of local savings tends to seek safer haven abroad.

Private investment, particularly foreign investment, is regarded with suspicion in many quarters. A great many and probably a majority of the citizens of hemisphere nations regard United States private investment as a form of exploitation or economic colonialism. There is a widespread, mistaken view that such investment takes more out of the area than it contributes to it. Fear of domination by United States companies is expressed frequently.

The central problem is the failure of governments throughout the hemisphere to recognize fully the importance of private investment. Thus realistic steps have not been taken to encourage private investment, to create a framework within which it can operate and which assures that it will serve the best interests of the entire community. Yet history shows that democratic societies which have provided such encouragement and such a framework have been the most successful in attaining their broad objectives.

United States government tax laws and regulations offer a number of significant barriers to private investment abroad. They make it impossible for local governments to offer effective tax incentives to United States investors. They discourage joint ventures—a form of investment viewed with favor in many parts of the hemisphere. Furthermore, the United States offers little in the way of positive incentives to encourage its investors to engage in enterprises elsewhere in the hemisphere.

Recommendation: National Policy Objective

The United States should provide maximum encouragement for private investment throughout the hemisphere.

Recommendations for Action

1. *The United States should not, for narrow domestic reasons, apply tax rules to United States private overseas investment which controvert efforts by developing nations to encourage private investment and promote joint ventures.*
   a. United States companies should not have to pay into the United States Treasury the difference be-

U.S. DIRECT INVESTMENT, 1960-1967

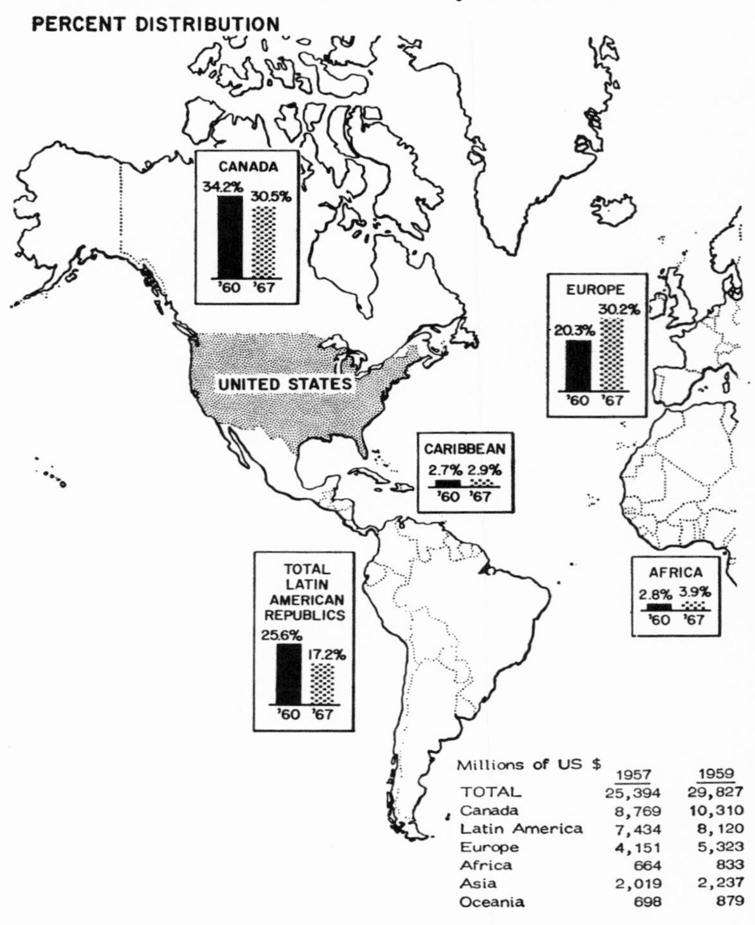

Millions of US $	1957	1959
TOTAL	25,394	29,827
Canada	8,769	10,310
Latin America	7,434	8,120
Europe	4,151	5,323
Africa	664	833
Asia	2,019	2,237
Oceania	698	879

Source: Survey of Current Business

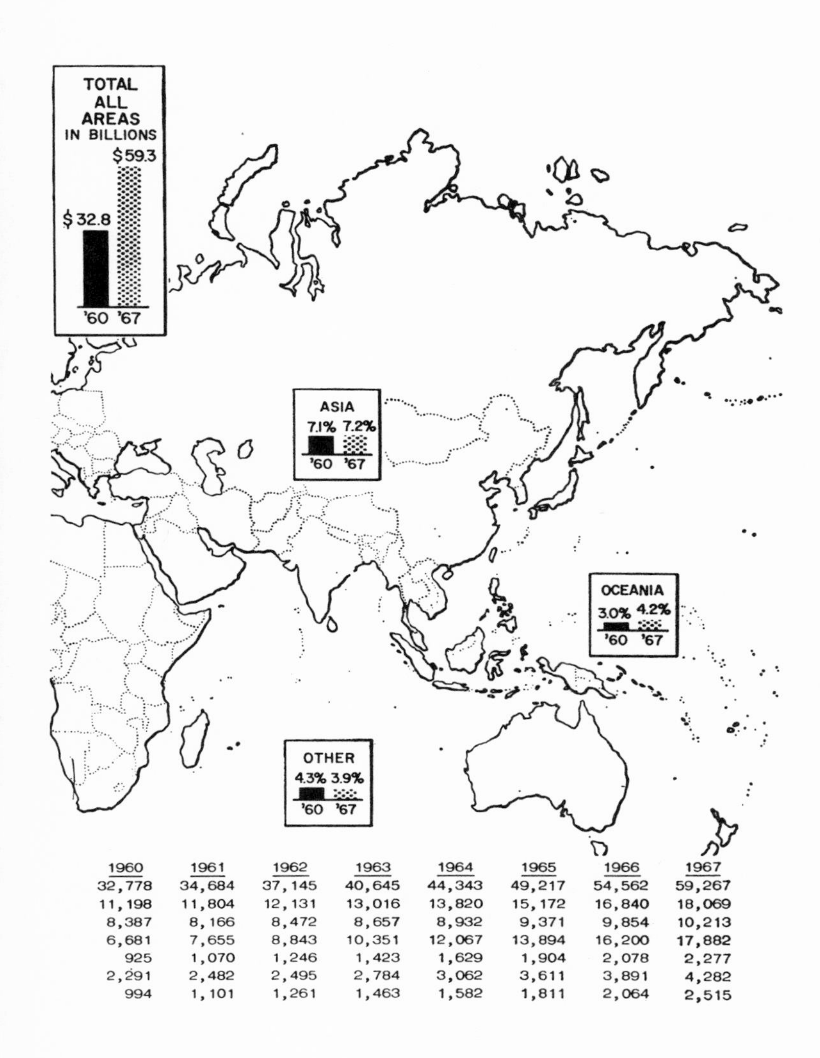

1960	1961	1962	1963	1964	1965	1966	1967
32,778	34,684	37,145	40,645	44,343	49,217	54,562	59,267
11,198	11,804	12,131	13,016	13,820	15,172	16,840	18,069
8,387	8,166	8,472	8,657	8,932	9,371	9,854	10,213
6,681	7,655	8,843	10,351	12,067	13,894	16,200	17,882
925	1,070	1,246	1,423	1,629	1,904	2,078	2,277
2,291	2,482	2,495	2,784	3,062	3,611	3,891	4,282
994	1,101	1,261	1,463	1,582	1,811	2,064	2,515

U.S. PRIVATE DIRECT INVESTMENT BY SELECTED INDUSTRIES IN LATIN AMERICAN REPUBLICS

PERCENT OF TOTAL

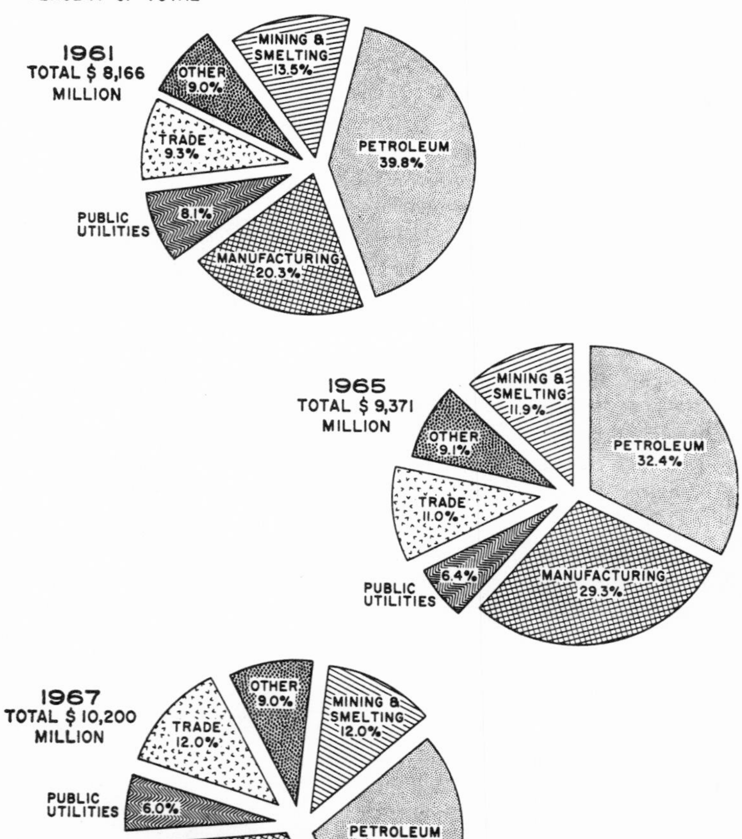

Source: U.S. Department of Commerce, Survey of Current Business

tween the United States corporate income tax and any lower tax assessed locally.

b. United States companies with minority holdings in foreign joint ventures should be able to consolidate returns from such ventures and offset any losses from them against parent company losses.

2. *Greater use should be made of the contract mechanism to bring private investors into ventures with discouragingly high risks but with the potential to make significant contributions to local economies.*

   a. The proposed Overseas Private Investment Corporation should have the power to contract with private companies in the Western Hemisphere to create production facilities necessary to meet an important need which is not being filled by private investors. In many cases, the problem is that the combinations of the capital required and the overhead costs involved in establishing a venture during its early years are so high as to make the venture unattractive even though longer-term prospects appear favorable. In such cases, the contract with the Overseas Private Investment Corporation would cover these start-up costs through some combination of loans and contract payments, possibly involving participation by multi-national, regional, or national development banks.

   b. Contracts should be worked out in a flexible fashion and could provide, for instance, that the participating private company would have an option to purchase an agreed-upon per cent of the equity once the venture was successful, with the remainder of the equity sold to local investors. Such a contract mechanism offers a direct and flexible approach toward encouraging a greater flow of private investment. It is better than the shotgun approach of tax incentives to U.S. private investment which, in reality, constitutes a form of subsidy.

3. *The proposal to transfer AID functions relating to private investment into a new corporation—the Overseas Private Investment Corporation—should be supported.*

a. Every effort should be made to form a private United States insurance group to take over insurance of private foreign investment under a reinsurance arrangement with the Overseas Private Investment Corporation.
   —This would further remove the U.S. government from direct involvement in protecting U.S. private investment.

4. *Improved mechanisms should be sought to bring together United States private investors and companies elsewhere in the hemisphere which are seeking United States partners.*
   a. The need for communication is particularly significant in the case of small and medium-sized United States companies which could make contributions in terms of capital and technical knowledge.
   b. This might be done through Joint Councils involving the United States Council for Latin America and local counterparts, perhaps with government support.
   c. The contract mechanism might be useful in certain cases in facilitating such joint ventures.
   d. It might be feasible to revive under the Organization of American States the Inter-American Development Commission with its country commissions to help in mobilizing the private sector.

5. *High priority should be given to the development and training of entrepreneurs, managers, scientists, and technicians.*
   a. The proposed Overseas Private Investment Corporation should be charged with the responsibility for actively promoting such efforts.
   b. U.S. companies should also provide support. Increased facilities for training both students and teachers in the United States should be a part of the program. The International Executive Service Corps is now doing outstanding work in this field.

6. *The United States should support all efforts to encourage local savings and to channel them into productive investment.*
   a. Regional and national development banks should be

supported by the United States with administrative, technical, and financial assistance.

b. The United States should support the development of local open-end investment trusts (i) to mobilize local savings for local industrial investment, and (ii) as a vehicle to utilize counterpart funds to finance local private participation in joint ventures with foreign capital for local industrial development. This could be a means of achieving greater local participation in joint ventures with United States companies.

c. Arrangements could be set up in which U.S. government loans would be used to finance in part the development of local and regional markets. One such experiment is now underway in Brazil with an AID loan. If successful, the pattern could be applied elsewhere.

d. To encourage local savings, the World Bank might issue bonds repayable in constant real value.

e. A Latin American dollar market (similar to the EuroDollar market) could be developed in which deposits denominated in dollars could be used to finance local development.

f. United States assistance funds could be used to guarantee part (e.g., 25 per cent) of loans made by local banks or other financial institutions to support rural village development projects such as water supply, grain storage, simple irrigation, housing, and farm-to-market access roads.

7. *The United States government should work with the proposed Western Hemisphere Development Committee and with representatives from the private sectors to develop a set of uniform rules of conduct for private foreign investment.*

    a. Such rules should cover the behavior of both private companies and host governments.

    b. Private enterprise flourishes under a system of reasonable and predictable rules of the game involving a minimum of red tape.

    c. A greater identification between the policies of private foreign investors and the national interest of host countries is required. Such problems can best be worked out on a hemisphere-wide basis.

5. Urban Development and Housing

Adequate housing and improved conditions of urban living stand high on the list of factors which contribute to the quality of life throughout the Western Hemisphere. Yet in large part because of a continuing influx of people from rural areas, cities are falling behind in providing the conditions and services which make them reasonably safe and decent places in which to work and live.

Housing needs far exceed the available supply of medium- and low-cost facilities. Of the population moving into cities, a high percentage live in slums. This causes not only difficult housing and health problems but also unprecedented structural change. Extreme traffic congestion is seen everywhere. Health facilities are inadequate and sanitary and water supply systems are presently insufficient. The very high urban population growth rate (more than 50 per cent higher than the rate of growth in total population) exceeds the increase in job opportunities, so unemployment is generally high and rising, particularly among the young.

In confronting these massive problems, most of which have intensified greatly in the past decade, municipal administration has been swamped. Financial requirements are staggering and go well beyond presently available funds from archaic urban tax systems and aid from central governments.

These problems of urban development are universal in the Western Hemisphere. Major cities in the United States face much the same difficulties as do cities elsewhere. It will require the combined experience and cooperative efforts of people and governments throughout the Western Hemisphere to accelerate progress in dealing with urban problems.

It is increasingly clear that what is needed is a systems approach to community development. Specific elements—such as transportation, schools, housing, sanitary facilities, administration, and finance—must be integrated into a cohesive approach within the context of national, regional, and urban planning. Rural and urban development need to be considered as integral partners in overall national development. Factors

HOUSING DEFICITS* (IN THOUSANDS OF UNITS)

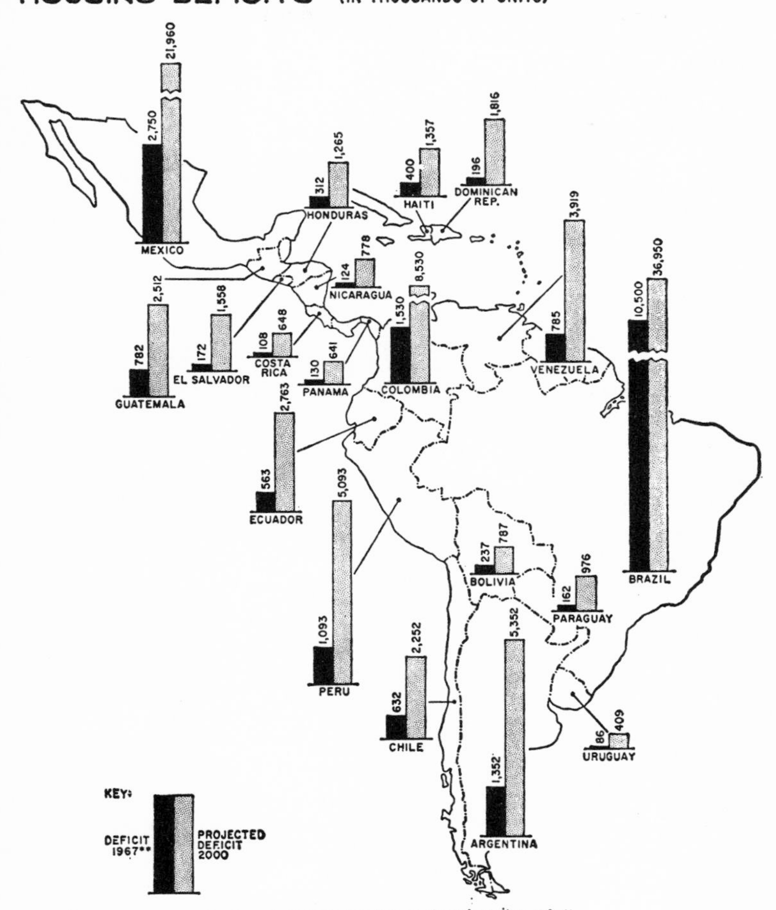

*Figures are intended only as indicators of Latin America's Housing deficit.
**Or latest available year.

HOUSING
1960 OR LATEST AVAILABLE DATA

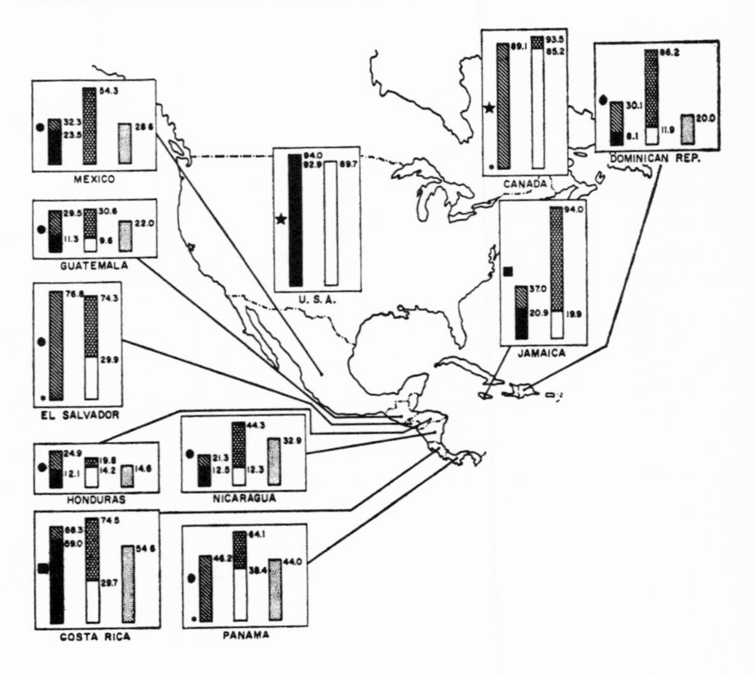

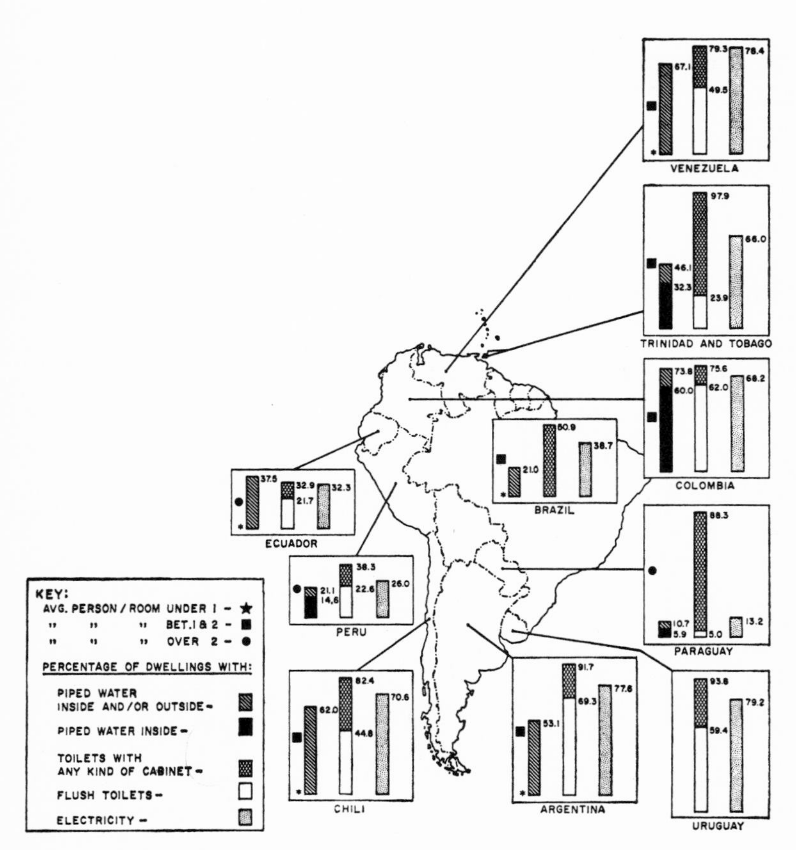

Source: United Nations, Statistical Abstract of the United States, 1968

*Data on % of piped water inside not available but is included in total % with piped water.

influencing the migratory flows between rural and urban areas need to be given priority study and attention. Both agricultural and industrial development should proceed on a balanced basis.

While much has been learned about the complex problems involved in improving housing and urban conditions, much more remains to be learned. This is a hemisphere-wide challenge. It is also a compelling opportunity to work together, to learn together, to deal imaginatively and effectively with common problems.

RECOMMENDATION: NATIONAL POLICY OBJECTIVE

The United States should give maximum feasible support to urban and rural community development to improve housing and a broad range of community services so as to elevate the quality of the environment in which people live.

RECOMMENDATIONS FOR ACTION

1. *The United States should undertake a major program for the rehabilitation of its own cities. This will meet the essential needs of our own people; it will demonstrate to other American republics that this job can be done and it will establish the legitimacy of our own system and its ability to set essential priorities.*
2. *United States assistance efforts in the other American republics must be broadened in orientation to total community development.*
   —Whereas some of the other countries are beginning to work to meet the needs for social self-help and self-determination of low-income groups, U.S. assistance programs are still oriented at the physical and material environment and not at total social, educational, and community development.
3. *The U.S. housing loan guarantee and loan programs should be improved.*
   —While important in individual cases, these loan programs are small in relation to the total problem, and they are frequently not integrated into broad urban and rural development plans. However, as a general

rule, the funds to finance housing and urban development should be generated locally.

4. *United States programs should stress efforts to join together with local private sector groups, municipal and national governments, and regional and hemisphere organizations in seeking new ways to improve the environment in both urban and rural areas.*
5. *The United States should also help in the development of mechanisms which will promote individual savings and direct them into housing and other community facilities.*
   a. Seed capital can be provided to help establish local institutions which will provide safe and attractive places in which individuals can deposit their savings.
   b. These institutions can use such funds to finance housing and urban improvements.
   c. Where there is a problem of inflation, arrangements can be worked out to safeguard the value of individual savings by relating both the return to savers and the payments by borrowers to an agreed-upon index of prices.

D. The Division of Labor

In essence, what we the people of the Western Hemisphere really need is a more efficient division of labor among us.

The division of labor is one of the tried and true economic principles that will be as valid in 1976 as it was in 1776 when it was first spelled out by Adam Smith. His example involved the manufacture of dress pins in which some eighteen distinct operations were required. When one man had to perform all eighteen operations, he "could certainly not make twenty pins a day," said Adam Smith. But if the process could be divided up so that eighteen people specialized, with each one performing one particular function of the process, the total output per person could be raised to as much as 4,800 pins per day, according to Adam Smith.

This principle of the division of labor underlies the progress of modern nations. Within national boundaries, the forces of competition in the market lead to specialization—a division of labor. Individuals and companies turn to what they can produce most effectively because that yields the greatest returns. Thus one company will concentrate on the production of ax handles while another will specialize in producing ax heads. The result will be better axes, lower prices to consumers, and higher returns to workers and employers.

The same principles apply internationally. All participants gain from the freest possible exchange of exports and imports, since that promotes an international division of labor. Each nation concentrates on items it can produce with relatively greater efficiency and lowest costs. It trades these items for those which other nations can produce with selectively greater efficiency. Everyone gains in the process, just as they do in the division of labor within national boundaries.

What is needed now is a broadening division of labor among the nations of the Western Hemisphere. At present, the United States is producing, at high cost behind tariff walls and quotas, goods which could be produced more economically by other hemisphere nations. The U.S. is short of skilled labor and, if anything, this shortage promises to get worse. The shortage of skilled labor is intensified when the U.S. continues to keep workers in lines which are, by definition, inefficient, since production can only be carried on here behind tariff or quota barriers. National productivity would be enhanced by shifting workers and capital out of protected industries into industries where advanced technology and intensive capital investment permits the U.S. to pay high wages and still remain competitive in world markets. The goods the United States is now producing inefficiently would be imported, mainly from less developed countries. Consumers would gain through lower prices, workers would receive higher wages, and the return on capital would be higher.

The less-developed countries would also gain. With abundant supplies of labor and wage levels well below those in the United States, they could export processed foods, textiles, apparel, footwear, and other light manufactures, as well as meat and other farm products. This would provide increased employment at higher wages than are now available. Workers could move off farms into higher paid industrial jobs. The increase in income would raise living standards generally, contributing to the improvement in the quality of life. Such nations would become better customers for the high-technology products of the United States.

In a real sense, the failure to develop a full division of labor in the Western Hemisphere can be termed inhumane. The excess production of certain farm products and raw materials in the less-developed countries results from protectionism in the industrial nations which slows the pace of industrialization in the less-developed nations. With overproduction, prices of such farm products and raw materials sink to levels which yield no more than a bare subsistence return to most of the individuals producing them.

It has been objected in some quarters of the United States that the adjustments involved in a move toward a greater international division of labor would prove too painful to be borne. There would be adjustments, and an effective program would be needed to help affected workers and businesses to make the transition to more productive pursuits.

Yet experience suggests that the adjustment process would be amazingly smooth if tariffs and quotas were phased out over a reasonable period. The European Economic Community eliminated all barriers to trade in industrial products over a seven-year period with few perceptible difficulties. The massive reductions in U.S. tariffs, from their towering heights under the Smoot-Hawley tariff act in 1930, have had beneficial effects. A healthy domestic economy can absorb adjustments to increased imports with little disruption and with benefits to all.

Recommendation: National Policy Objective

The President should request the Organization of American States to convene a major hemisphere conference to establish a more rational division of labor in the hemisphere.

The Western Hemisphere Development Committee could take responsibility for the preparatory arrangements and agenda for such a conference. After the conference, that same Committee could be given the responsibility for following through on the conference conclusions and programs.

Such a conference should be composed of representatives of all concerned sectors—legislative and executive branches of governments, business, labor unions, agricultural producers, and consumers.

In the long run, such a conference might well prove to be a real beginning for a new crusade to elevate the dignity of the individual and the quality of life in the Western Hemisphere.

E. Education, Science, and Culture

The quality of life in any nation today is fundamentally related to the level of its science and the vitality of its culture. Both, in turn, are crucially dependent on education.

A good educational system is absolutely essential to produce the trained leadership required for scholarship, public affairs, the creative arts, management, science, modern agricultural production, and skilled industrial labor. No nation ever has had enough highly trained people to meet all of its needs. This lack has been especially severe in the less industrialized nations of the Western Hemisphere.

The educational problems in many of the American republics are critical; there are others, however, with advanced educational systems. In the aggregate, out of 108 million children between five and twenty years of age in 1965, 65 million were not enrolled in schools. Dropout rates average 70 per cent for primary schools and 65 per cent at the secondary level.

The individuals who take courses in the university constitute only 4 per cent of the total age group, and of those, still fewer receive university degrees. The greatest educational needs are at the secondary level and higher levels, due in large part to the emphasis on the expansion of primary education apparent since 1961.

Opportunities for study, research, and observation in the United States have developed a growing number of highly qualified leaders in all fields in the American republics. This is especially true in the critically important fields of education, agriculture, economics, government, the sciences and engineering, trade and industry, and the arts—fields in which opportunities for advanced training in most of the American republics are exceedingly limited.

STUDENTS AS A PERCENT OF SCHOOL-AGE POPULATION
(DATA IN THOUSANDS)

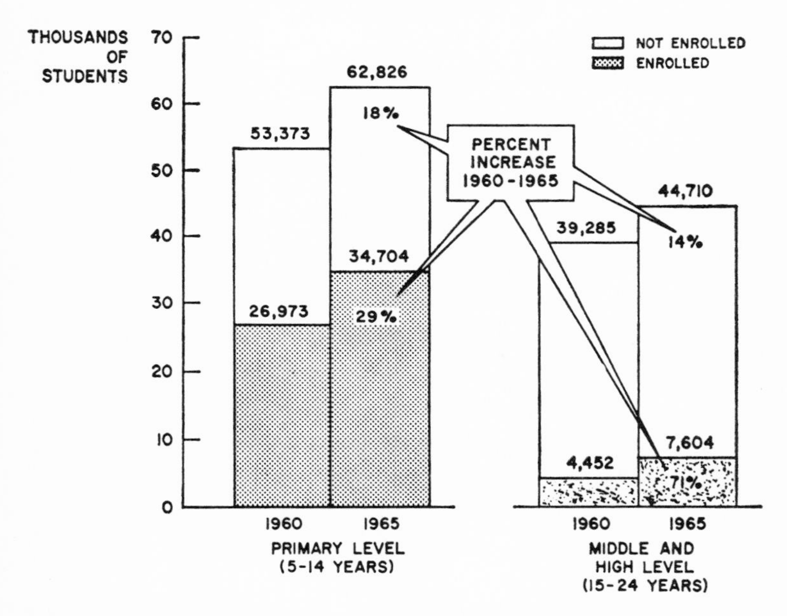

NOTE: IN NORTH AMERICA, THERE WERE 43.6 MILLION CHILDREN AGED 5-14 IN 1965, OF WHICH 87% WERE ENROLLED IN SCHOOLS. OF 33.8 MILLION AGED 15-24, 60% WERE STUDENTS.

SOURCE: U.N.E.C.O STATISTICAL YEARBOOK 1967

EDUCATIONAL PROBLEMS CONFRONTING THE HEMISPHERE

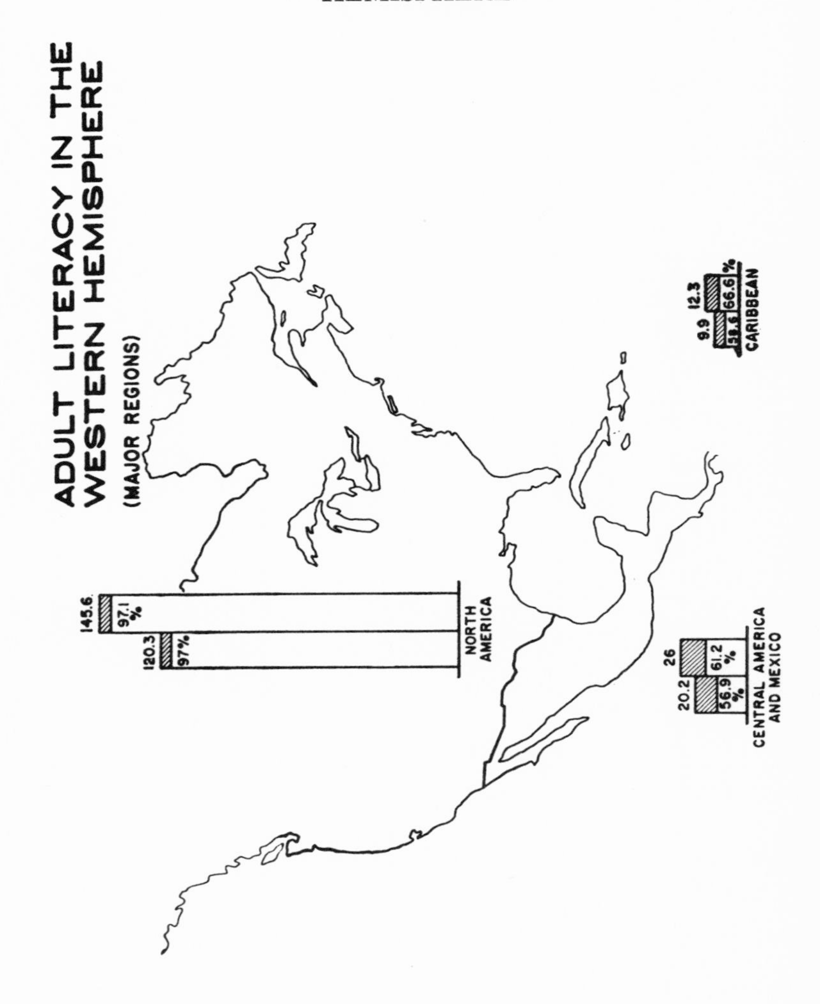

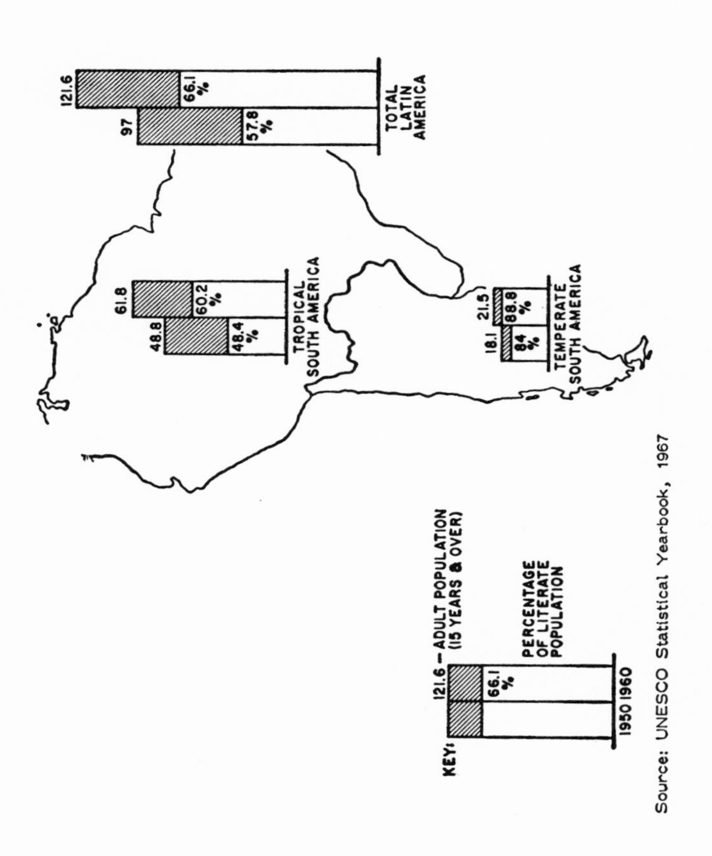
121.6
97
66.1 %
57.8 %
TOTAL LATIN AMERICA
61.8
48.8
60.2 %
48.4 %
TROPICAL SOUTH AMERICA
21.5
18.1
88.8 %
84 %
TEMPERATE SOUTH AMERICA
KEY:
121.6 — ADULT POPULATION (15 YEARS & OVER)
66.1 %
PERCENTAGE OF LITERATE POPULATION
1950 1960
Source: UNESCO Statistical Yearbook, 1967

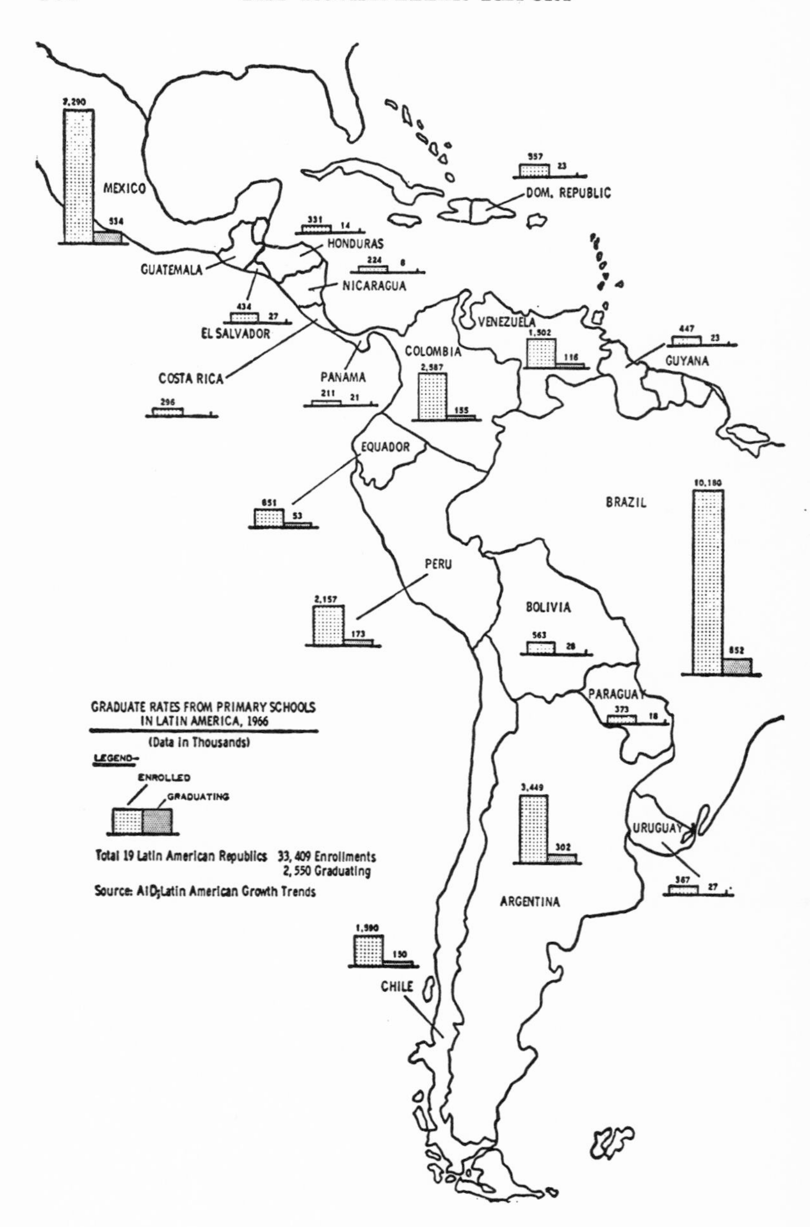
7,290
MEXICO
534
357
23
DOM. REPUBLIC
331
14
HONDURAS
224
8
NICARAGUA
GUATEMALA
434
27
EL SALVADOR
COSTA RICA
296
PANAMA
211
21
VENEZUELA
1,502
116
COLOMBIA
2,587
155
447
23
GUYANA
EQUADOR
651
53
BRAZIL
10,180
852
PERU
2,157
173
BOLIVIA
563
28
PARAGUAY
373
18
GRADUATE RATES FROM PRIMARY SCHOOLS
IN LATIN AMERICA, 1966
(Data in Thousands)
LEGEND—
ENROLLED
GRADUATING
Total 19 Latin American Republics 33,409 Enrollments
2,550 Graduating
Source: AID;Latin American Growth Trends
3,449
302
URUGUAY
367
27
ARGENTINA
1,990
150
CHILE

PERCENTAGE DISTRIBUTION
OF ENROLLED STUDENTS

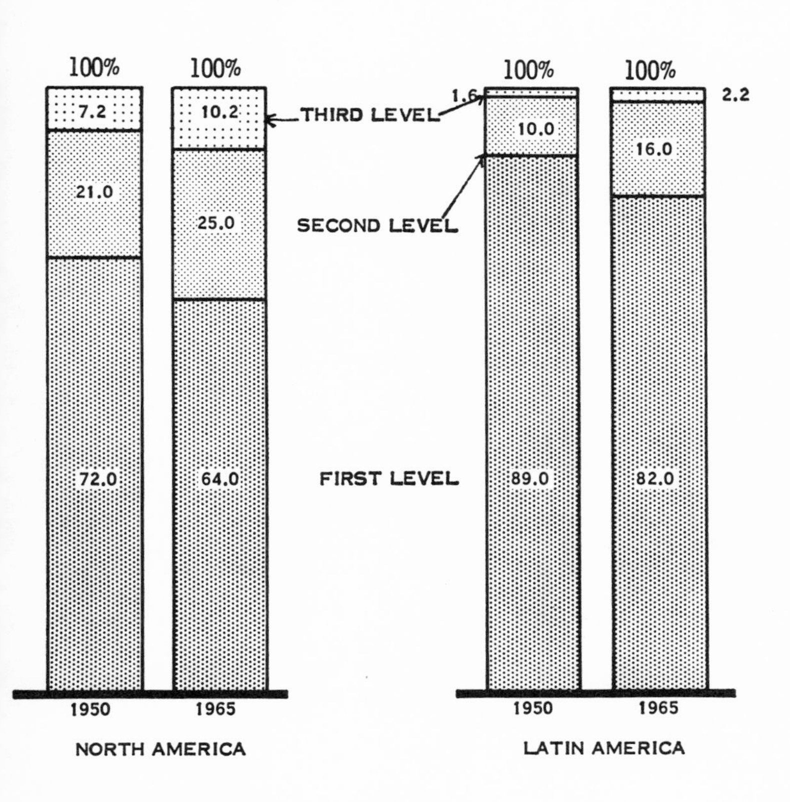

SOURCE– UNESCO STATISTICAL YEARBOOK 1967

NUMBER OF THIRD LEVEL STUDENTS PER 100,000

IN 1965 OR LATEST AVAILABLE YEAR

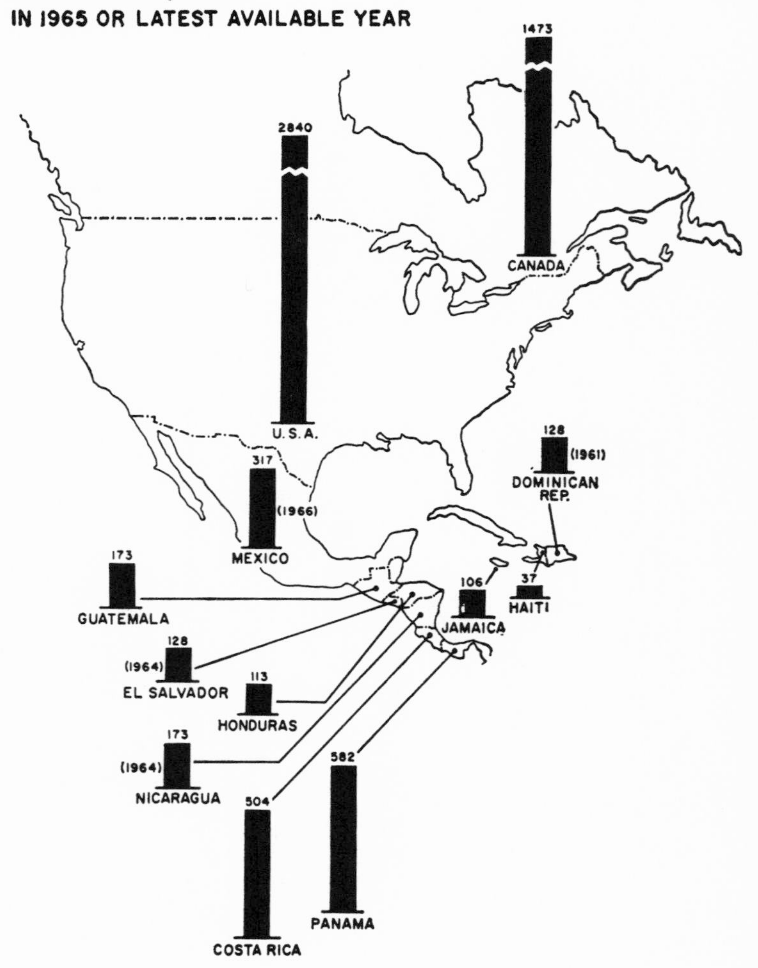

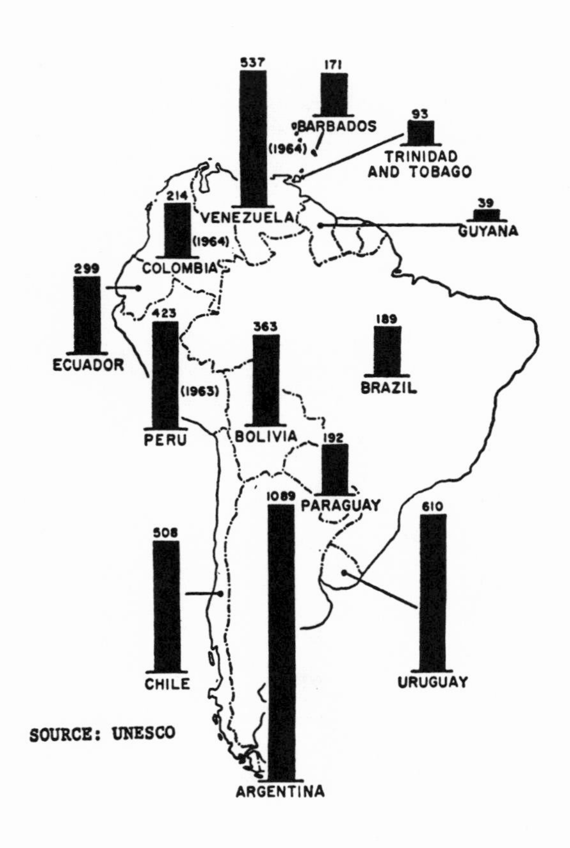
537
171
BARBADOS
(1964)
93
TRINIDAD
AND TOBAGO
214
VENEZUELA
39
GUYANA
(1964)
COLOMBIA
299
423
363
189
ECUADOR
(1963)
BRAZIL
PERU
BOLIVIA
192
1089
PARAGUAY
610
508
CHILE
URUGUAY
SOURCE: UNESCO
ARGENTINA

PUBLIC EXPENDITURE ON EDUCATION AS PERCENT OF NATIONAL INCOME

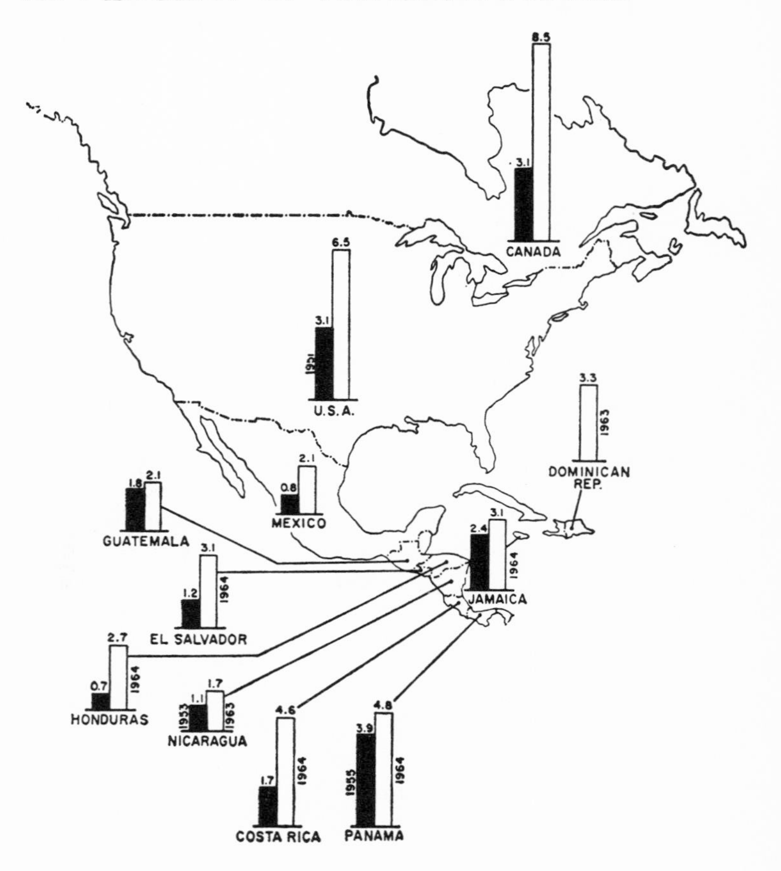

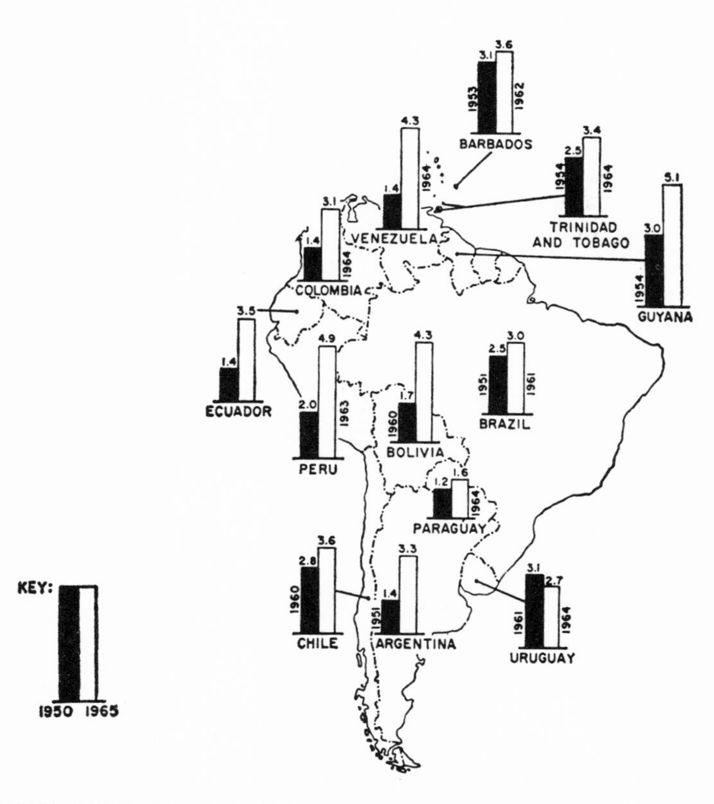

Source: UNESCO Statistical Yearbook, 1967

Until recently, however, there has been little appreciation of the need and value of scientific and technical competence among those who determine national policies and set national priorities in other hemisphere countries. Encouragement and support for scientific education or for scientific research or for laboratories and research institutes have also been lacking. The use of scientists and engineers in schools and colleges, in government, and in the private sectors of agriculture and industry has been inadequate.

These factors have had a direct bearing on the health, development, and character of each of the Western Hemisphere nations.

Out of scientific research flow new products and processes, new medicine, and new leisure. More than this, science colors the culture of a nation and directly affects the health of its people and the productivity of its agriculture. In a considerable measure, science determines the vitality of a nation's industrial economy—and it is basic to its military security.

Science, however, is only one part of culture. It functions, it is nourished, and it contributes in interrelationship with the total culture of a nation—its creative arts, its social sciences, its human and ethical values. Support of science must therefore neither exclude the encouragement of these other essential elements of a nation's culture, nor be disproportionate.

What is needed is a focal point in government to harness the concern for educational, scientific, and cultural development in the Western Hemisphere into one agency. In recognition of this need, the Organization of American States in the Protocol of Buenos Aires is currently proposing a new Council for Education, Science and Culture to support initiatives in these fields throughout the hemisphere.

By contrast, in the United States, responsibility in these fields remains dispersed in a number of government agencies. It should be centralized in a new government institute, having corporate form and powers, which could enlist some of the most distinguished heads of the nation's outstanding educational, scientific, and cultural institutions as members of its board of directors. The objective of such an institute would be to mount a major effort to correct the previous neglect of these fields which are crucial to the vitality and welfare of the hemisphere.

The Western Hemisphere has had a uniquely rich cultural life in pre-Colombian, colonial, and modern times. Increased cultural interchange will foster increasing mutual appreciation and respect. Neither art nor science knows national boundaries, They are, rather, the bridges linking the people of all nations, wherever situated and whatever their form of government, in understanding and friendship.

RECOMMENDATION: NATIONAL POLICY OBJECTIVE

The United States should give full support to the objectives of the new Council for Education, Science and Culture of the Organization of American States.

RECOMMENDATIONS FOR ACTION

In order to support the new Organization of American States Council's purposes, the United States should make a major commitment by creating a new corporation, with financing in the magnitude of $100 million annually to start with. The majority of its board of directors would be outstanding heads of private institutions. It would be known as the WESTERN HEMISPHERE INSTITUTE FOR EDUCATION, SCIENCE AND CULTURE, *and would be an operating arm of the Economic and Social Development Agency.*

In order to carry out its mission, such an institute should be authorized to:

1. Foster effective systems of elementary education by encouraging the creation of demonstration schools that encompass the elements of modern science and the structure of modern society, including the principles of social science and the nature of human aspiration;
2. Help establish regional universities to provide leadership in the training of men and women of high ability;
3. Help identify and support with scholarships and fellowships the able young men and women who might otherwise not be able to develop to a high level their latent skills, ability, and adventurous talent;
4. Encourage the exchange among the hemisphere nations of men and women—students, technicians, teachers,

journalists, artists, and professionals—in all fields of endeavor;
5. Support the utilization of new educational techniques such as the use of radio and television for elementary education in rural areas;
6. As literacy is increased, assist in improving the availability and quality of public libraries;
7. Expand hemisphere cultural activities in the visual and performing arts as well as the humanities and experiment with new and imaginative approaches—such as the appointment of creative people as cultural officers in United States embassies, forming a cultural corps on the pattern of the Peace Corps, arranging for youth festivals to tour the hemisphere, and encouraging the production of folk art for export to the United States;
8. Support the establishment of regional institutes for basic scientific research; and,
9. Encourage local and international corporations to allocate a larger percentage of their resources and effort to scientific research as part of their operations in the hemisphere.

F. Labor

The key to progress in any country is its work force. Organized labor is and will continue to be a major factor in enhancing the quality of life in the Western Hemisphere.

In their own efforts to make economic and social advances, free trade-union movements in the hemisphere nations are directing their efforts toward increasing the productivity of industry and increasing labor's share of industrial productivity.

Opposed to the hemisphere free trade unions are the communist-dominated unions. These political unions called for general strikes in almost every country the mission visited, to prevent or protest its arrival, but democratic trade unions refused to go along with them.

In most hemisphere countries, labor is now excluded from government planning for development. This has caused widespread frustration among labor leaders, who feel their governments show little concern for the role of organized labor and little concern about low wages, poor working conditions, and unemployment. From the nation's standpoint, labor's lack of involvement in planning means that workers and unions cannot make their maximum contribution to economic development.

Except for four hemisphere countries, there are no reliable statistics about unemployment, underemployment, wage levels, costs of living, and other data that concern the worker. Unemployment is known to be high in most hemisphere countries, but the lack of precise statistical data handicaps efforts to deal with the problem.

Industrial development is being retarded in many countries because of a shortage of skilled workers, due to the lack of a literate work force and to the shortage of facilities for vocational and technical training.

RECOMMENDATION: NATIONAL POLICY OBJECTIVE

The United States should encourage strong, effective, free trade-union movements throughout the Western Hemisphere.

RECOMMENDATIONS FOR ACTION

1. *The United States should encourage governments of the hemisphere to include labor representation in planning their programs for development.*
2. *The United States should increase its financial and technical assistance, through the American Institute for Free Labor Development, for worker education and vocational training in the other hemisphere countries.*

G. Agriculture

To the twenty-four nations of Central America, the Caribbean, and South America, agriculture is a dominant fact of life. For a majority of the peoples of these nations, the quality of life itself is dependent on the farm. On the average, nearly half the labor force of the other American nations is in agriculture, fishing, or forestry.

RURAL POPULATION AS PERCENTAGE OF TOTAL POPULATION

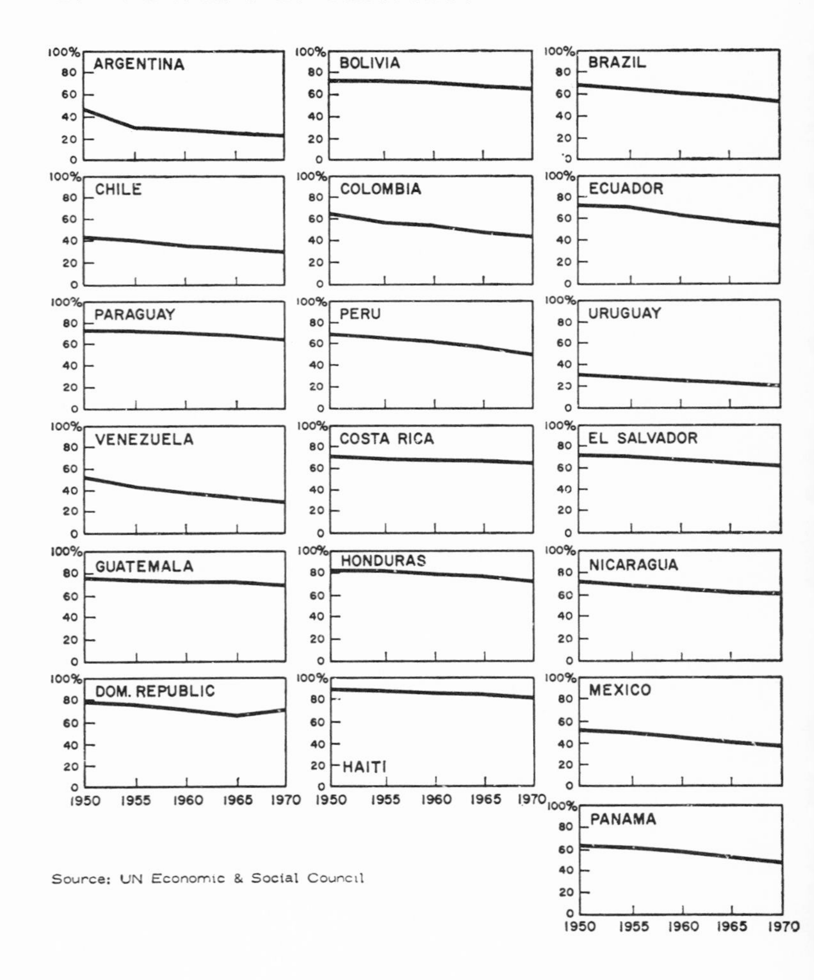

Source: UN Economic & Social Council

ECONOMICALLY ACTIVE POPULATION BY SECTORS IN LATIN AMERICA

PERCENTAGE DISTRIBUTION

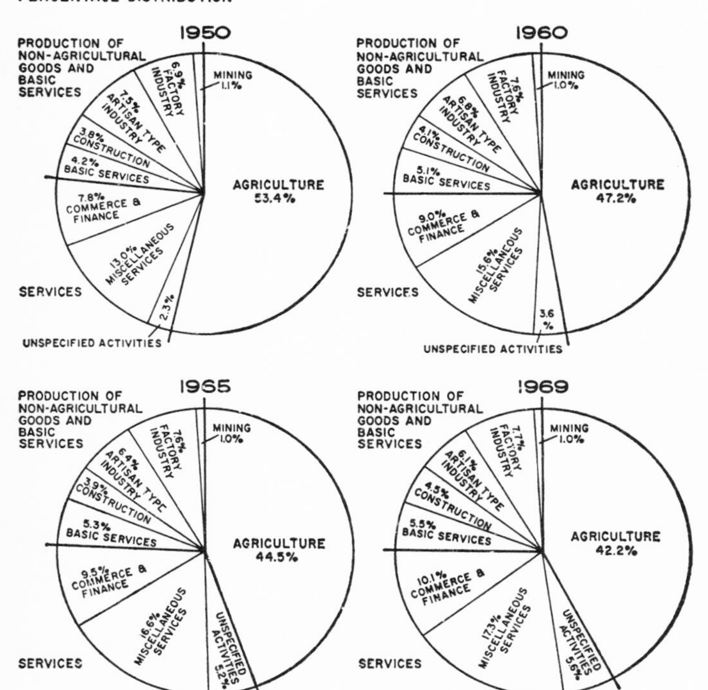

ECONOMICALLY ACTIVE POPULATION AS PERCENTAGE OF TOTAL POPULATION

	1950	1960	1965	1969 EST.
AGRICULTURE	18.3	15.8	14.7	13.9
MINING	.4	.3	.3	.3
FACTORY INDUSTRY	2.3	2.5	2.5	2.6
ARTISAN TYPE IND.	2.6	2.3	2.1	2.0
CONSTRUCTION	1.3	1.4	1.3	1.5
BASIC SERVICES	1.4	1.7	1.8	1.8
COMM. & FINANCE	2.7	3.0	3.2	3.3
MISC. SERVICES	4.4	5.2	5.5	5.7
UNSPECIFIED ACTIVITIES	0.8	1.2	1.7	1.9
TOTAL	34.2	33.4	33.1	33.0

Source: UN Economic & Social Council

To those who live as subsistence farmers, life is a struggle for existence on the land—with a burro, a machete, a crude hut, and a small hoard of maize and beans patiently coaxed from the soil. These millions live outside any national economy—and they live with the bleak realization that, as things are, there will never be a better life for them.

Yet there is great potential wealth in the good earth of the hemisphere. The grasslands of South America are one of the greatest sources of animal protein in the world. The tropical forests of the hemisphere represent one of the earth's largest remaining timber reserves. A vast expanse of the richest land in all the world lies in a broad belt on the eastern slopes of the Andes. In addition, entire countries and great regions are blessed with good soil and abundant sunshine, ample water and dependable growing seasons. With existing modern scientific and technical knowledge, the other American nations *could* become one of the great food baskets of the world.

Despite this great potential, and the impact in some countries of hybrid seeds on increased yields per acre, these nations taken as a group do not now produce enough food inexpensively to feed their own peoples properly. While overall food production is going up, food production per person, due to the population explosion, is estimated at 10 per cent less than it was at the end of World War II. And each year there are eight million more mouths to feed—an annual increase equivalent to the population of New York City.

Individual countries and areas have attained highly industrialized agricultural production. As a whole, however, agriculture is slipping further and further behind its great promise.

The reasons for this include poor living conditions and little education for rural people; inefficient use of land; inequitable distribution of land; inadequate credit and extension services; lack of basic and applied agricultural research; too few farm-to-market roads and too few trucks for moving agricultural products; low and uncertain prices for products; lack of packaging, storage, and marketing facilities; and lack of nutrition and good health, initiative, imagination, and agricultural management—all of which, in turn, are chiefly caused by poverty and lack of education.

The end results include not only malnutrition with all its crippling effects on human energies and intellectual capacities,

INDEX OF AGRICULTURAL PRODUCTION

——— PER CAPITA - - - - - - TOTAL

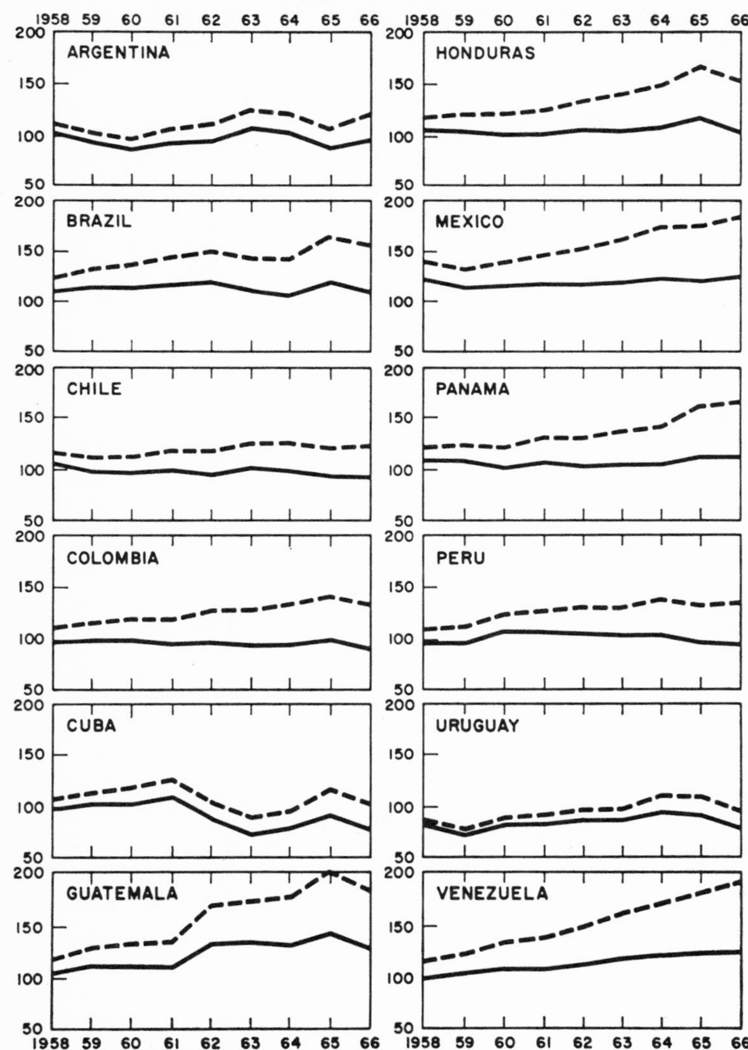

Source: FAO Production Yearbook, Vol. 21, 1967

Calculated on a uniform basis employing regionally constant weights.

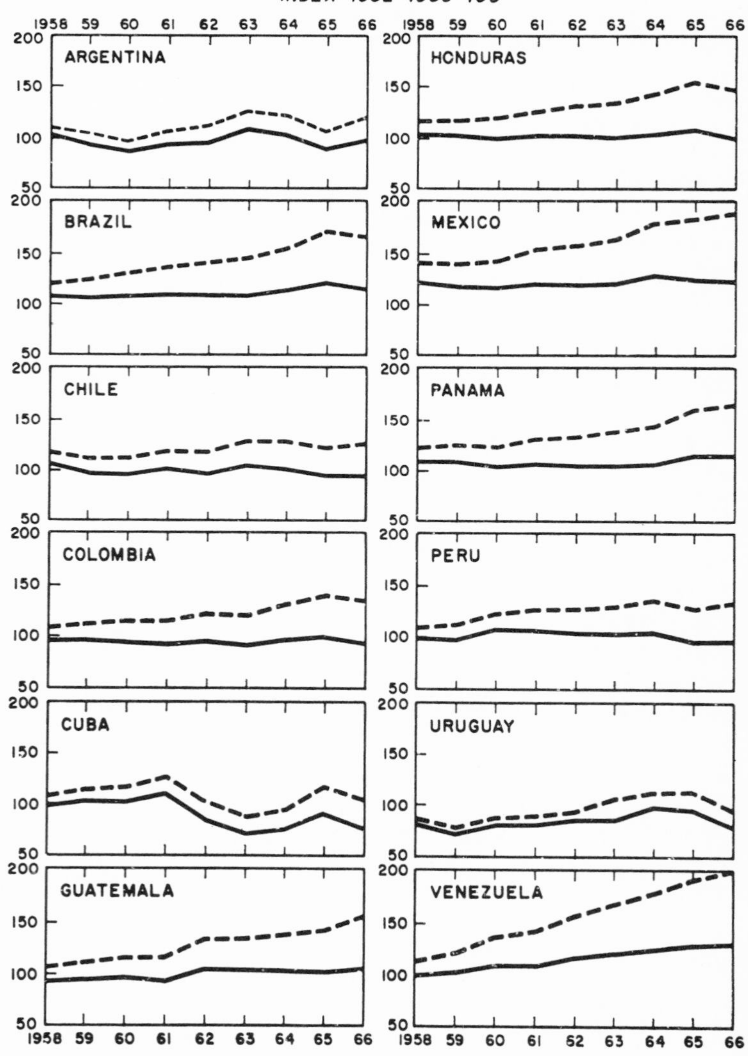

Source: FAO Production Yearbook, Vol. 21, 1967

Calculated on a uniform basis employing regionally constant weights.

but also a flood tide of desperate migration from rural areas to city slums.

Yet our discussions brought forth the central fact that all the countries we visited see agriculture as the foundation force for raising their own standards of living, creating employment opportunities, and generating foreign exchange and capital for economic and social development.

One of the adverse forces in this situation is the refusal of the United States to give these countries of the Western Hemisphere sufficient access to United States markets for their agricultural products. This fact highlights the fundamental inconsistency between our policies of economic aid and our policies of trade.

On the one hand, the U.S. government, especially through AID, has encouraged the countries to diversify their agriculture and produce beef, tomatoes, cotton, wheat, corn, rice, and other products. On the other hand, the same U.S. government, through orders issued by the Agriculture Department and restrictions imposed by Congress, prohibits and limits exports of these products so as to protect United States prices and producers.

Throughout history, agricultural growth has been essential to the general progress of every nation and every civilization. If the nations of the Western Hemisphere are to make the great progress of which they are capable, they must make the most of their greatest assets—land, water, climate, and people anxious to be trained—by using the hybrid seeds, the chemicals and equipment to grow food cheaply and abundantly, which have been developed in the last two decades. The other Americas have no alternative to expanding agricultural production. As a minimum, they must boost it by 4 to 5 per cent a year just to keep up with current population growth and to improve diets.

Recommendation: National Policy Objective

The United States should recognize that improvement of rural life and increasing agricultural production are basic to improvement of the quality of life in the Western Hemisphere.

RECOMMENDATIONS FOR ACTION

1. *The United States should make a concerted effort through program and project loans and technical assistance to help our neighbors in their efforts to improve life in rural areas, to expand employment opportunities, and to grow more food for themselves and for export.*
   a. Programs of rural development including agrarian reform appropriate to the needs of the country are essential to increased agricultural production and to improve the quality of life in rural areas.
   b. These programs also will provide expanding opportunities for work in the face of a rapidly growing population, and help to halt the flooding of overcrowded cities with economic refugees from the countryside.
2. *The United States should allocate a major part of future growth in its agricultural consumption to hemisphere nations and reexamine the present limitations on the flow of farm products into the U.S. market from our neighbors to the south.*
   —The self-defeating nature and ultimate danger of the protectionist trend in the United States need to be better understood by the people of the United States; otherwise, food prices will continue to rise and the adverse effect on the economic development of our neighbors will accelerate.
3. *The United States should undertake a series of agricultural demonstration programs at selected sites in different countries to serve both as examples and as a nucleus for further development in transforming subsistence farming into a dynamic factor for economic growth.*
   a. To carry this out, a nonprofit Inter-American Rural Development Corporation should be established as a subsidiary of the Institute of Western Hemisphere Affairs and should work with agricultural agencies in each country in establishing these pilot projects.
   b. Such projects would be operated by agricultural experts of the country concerned, with United States technical assistance. The idea would be to develop for each selected zone or region a working model of

the whole range of production, processing, and marketing services and facilities in an integrated and intensive operation.

H. Conservation

With few exceptions, the countries of Central America, South America, and the Caribbean lack effective resource conservation programs. With about three-fourths of the land area of these countries in some form of public ownership, there is up to the present no really effective protection or control over this so-called public domain.

Unless a program of protection and conservation of these resources is undertaken in the next few years, the pressures of a rapidly increasing population and uncontrolled resource exploitation will make it impossible for this to become a region of economically developed and self-supporting nations.

Of a 7,925,000-square-mile land area (compared with 3,549,000 square miles in the United States, including Alaska), one-half is covered with forests, one-quarter is made up of barren mountains, deserts, and other wild lands, and the remaining one-quarter is in grazing lands and only 5 per cent in cultivated crops—compared with 20 per cent in cultivated crops in the United States.

The food production base is largely confined to that 5 per cent of the total area in cultivated crops. This area is located mainly in hilly and mountainous country and is characterized by the most destructive type of shifting "fire and hoe" agriculture. There is little or no conservation practiced in the use of these lands.

The soils are largely tropical and complex in their makeup—and we still know very little about their proper management. While commercial, mechanized, and irrigation farming is expanding in the more level lands, and there are outstanding examples of soil conservation practices in many countries, the control of shifting agriculture and the development of alternative sources of livelihood for almost half the present farm population is a major problem.

The conservation of water resources is likewise almost completely neglected. There is hardly an urban center that does not have a water supply problem. Great hydroelectric power and irrigation schemes are being undertaken without proper measures to insure the conservation of watershed lands. The development of basic laws regulating water use is only now being given attention in many countries, and water pollution is particularly serious in the rapidly expanding urban areas.

Tropical forests represent one of the largest timber reserves in the world—one-fourth of the world's forest area. These forests are a basic though complex natural resource; very little is known about how to manage them properly. A part of this forest land area will be cleared in future years for farm crops and pastures, and in the process much valuable timber will be destroyed. A rational conservation program should permit the development of the best soils for agriculture but retain a forest cover on critical watershed lands, protect outstanding natural features as forested national parks and recreation areas, and manage commercial forests for the industrial development of lumber, pulpwood, and other forest products.

Grasslands, both natural and developed pasture lands, are potentially among the greatest sources of animal protein in the world because of the possibilities of year-round grazing use. The livestock industry is the most important branch of agriculture in many countries, but the conservation and improvement of grazing lands only now are beginning to be recognized as necessary to sustain the industry. There are also large areas of savanna and swamplands, deserts and sparsely vegetated mountain lands that need to be included in a program of wise use and conservation.

The rapid growth of human population and expanding settlement and opening up of the "backlands" is fast destroying birds, fish, and other wild animal life. It is to be expected that this will happen to some extent, but the situation is especially critical in Central and South America. Wild animals, birds, and fish are still a means of sustenance to the largely impoverished rural population and to the indigenous peoples of the "backland" areas. While there may be game laws in many countries, they are generally not enforced, as the need for them is little understood. At present, wildlife is regarded as an expendable resource, and without an organized consciousness in the population, especially among sportsmen and rural people, many species are bound to disappear.

Some of the most spectacular natural scenery in the world—the whole Andean mountain chain, the mountains of Mexico and Central America, Lake Titicaca, Iguazú and Angel Falls, the seashore areas of the Caribbean, and many others—may be found in these countries.

National parks and similar reserves have been created by several countries, but these are still insignificant in relation to the need. Outdoor recreation is only now coming into its own, and the need to develop adequate services and facilities for both domestic and international tourism is just now becoming apparent in many countries.

But in a few years the pressure of unrestricted use on many of these great natural areas will irreparably damage or destroy them. Now is the time to undertake a farsighted examination of the park and recreation needs, aimed at preserving the outstanding natural areas, the historical and cultural monuments, and wildlife species in danger of extinction.

Recommendation: National Policy Objective

The United States, through the combined resources of government and privately supported conservation agencies, should volunteer leadership and assistance for national and regional conservation programs wherever desired and feasible in the American republics.

Recommendations for Action

1. *Create an* Inter-American Institute of Natural Resource Conservation *within the framework of the Organization of American States.*
   a. Such an organization should have a board of directors made up of outstanding conservation leaders from all regions of the Americas.
   b. It would need substantial financing, largely from direct appropriations.
   c. It should have the technical advisory and training facilities of U. S. government and privately supported conservation agencies as backstopping for its program.

2. *The Conservation Institute should make a rapid reconnaissance survey of the American countries to classify and define the problem areas with regard to the destructive exploitation of soil, water, forests, grasslands, wildlife, and outstanding natural areas, and the need for conservation practices and controls.*
   —This should be followed by a program of investigation and research in natural resource use and management.
3. *A conservation education and information program should be launched, especially through the schools and in the rural areas.*
4. *A demonstration and training program in natural resource management and conservation should be inaugurated, especially for middle-level (non-university) personnel who will staff conservation projects and help establish control and protective measures over public lands.*
5. *A conservation public works program should be created, incorporating part of the Civilian Conservation Corps and Peace Corps approach with the part-time employment of peasant farmers.*

I. Health

The good health of the individual, wherever he lives, is fundamental to the quality of his life.

In the Western Hemisphere, significant improvements in public health have been made in the last quarter of a century. Smallpox, malaria, and yellow fever have been radically reduced. Yaws has been all but eradicated. For all these gains, infant mortality is appallingly high in the other American republics, malnutrition is increasing, and the lack of sanitation and water supply systems is the primary cause of intestinal parasites and other origins of sickness.

The population problem exacerbates all the other health problems through overcrowding in urban slums. It is so acute that the people themselves are promoting birth control.

In addition, the great increase of travel between the North and South American continents, the Central American countries, and the islands of the Caribbean has increasingly transformed the health problems of one country or region into the health problems of many areas.

Infant Mortality

As the 1968 annual report of the World Health Organization pointed out, as many as 20 per cent of the children born in some hemisphere countries die before they are five years old. This is the greatest single problem of health today in too many of the other American republics.

The Pan American Health Organization reported that in one recent year at least 741,000 child deaths in the other hemisphere nations should have been preventable. Of these deaths, 450,000 were under one year of age—and 291,000 were from one through four years of age.

Deaths of children under five years of age account for about 44 per cent of all deaths in Central and South America (as compared to 8 per cent for North America).

And one of the chief causes of these child deaths is contaminated water.

Water Is Life

The biggest cities of the Western Hemisphere for the most part do have potable water. And other Western Hemisphere cities with 250,000 and more people are building and operating municipal water systems through their own efforts and with the help of United States AID financial and technical assistance. The 1961 Alliance for Progress goal of supplying potable water by 1971 for 70 per cent of urban peoples is likely to be met, but the Alliance goal of doing the same for 50 per cent of the rural peoples will fall short by almost 10 percentage points.

At the present rate of progress, only 40 per cent to 50 per cent of the urban peoples in the other American republics may have potable water within the decade. For rural peoples, the outlook is that far fewer than 50 per cent will have potable water by 1971, the advisers were told.

"Don't build us hospitals; help us build water systems," a health officer in Brazil told the mission. "A child may be cured in a hospital, but with his next drink he is reinfected."

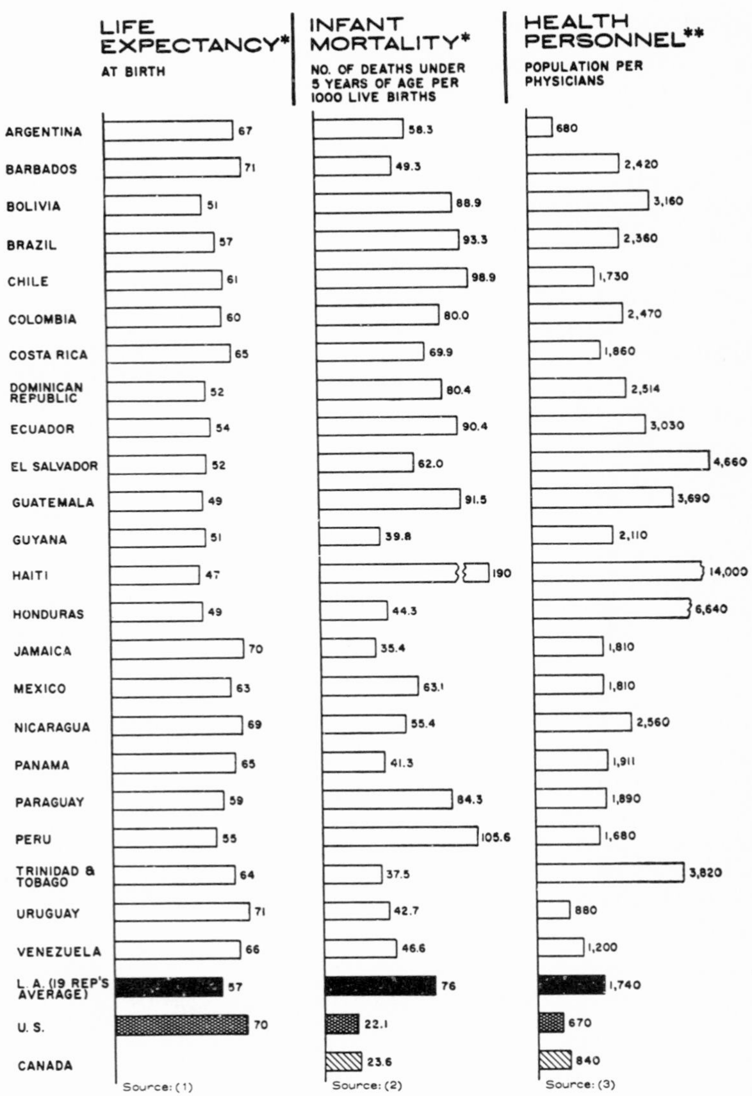

*1968 or latest available data **1967 or latest available data

(1) Source: AID-Economic Data Book; Social Progress Trust Fund; UN Demographic Yearbook
(2) Source: UN Demographic Yearbook; Social Progress Trust Fund; America en Cifras
(3) Source: UN Statistical Yearbook; AID-Economic Data Book, 1968

Legacy of Hunger

The *campesino* goes to bed hungry every night of his life. He will probably never see a doctor, a hospital, a dentist, or a nurse. He has little hope of being vaccinated against smallpox, or inoculated against typhoid, tetanus, or yellow fever. If he becomes ill, there is no medicine; he trusts to fate that he will either get better, or die.

The average citizen of Central and South America and the Caribbean can expect a life span of fifty-seven years, compared to seventy years for a North American.

Among the poor of most American countries, an expectant mother has so little to eat—and especially so little protein—that the child's physical and mental capabilities may be impaired even before he is born.

The Minister of Health of Brazil told the mission that undernourishment of an infant during the pre-natal period and first year of life can so weaken the brain cells that the child may never attain a normal capacity to learn. The Brazilian study confirms extensive studies made in the United States.

In one country a health official proposed that the U.S. Food for Peace school lunch program be taken away from seven- and eight-year-old children and shifted to a food program for expectant mothers.

"It may be too late to save this generation," the official said. "We should begin now to make sure the next generation reaches full physical and mental capacity."

Malnutrition blights much of South America, Central America, and the Caribbean countries. Only five nations maintain what the World Health Organization considers to be adequate as an average diet: 2,200 calories daily.

In Honduras, 70 per cent of the people are undernourished; in Haiti, more than 80 per cent.

Balance of Growth

Of all the broad concerns of the other Hemisphere nations, none is more compelling—in terms of public health, economic growth, and social progress—than the increase in population.

At the present extraordinary rate of increase, the number of people in the other American republics will more than

ESTIMATED PROTEIN AND CALORIE INTAKES AND DEFICITS - LATIN AMERICA

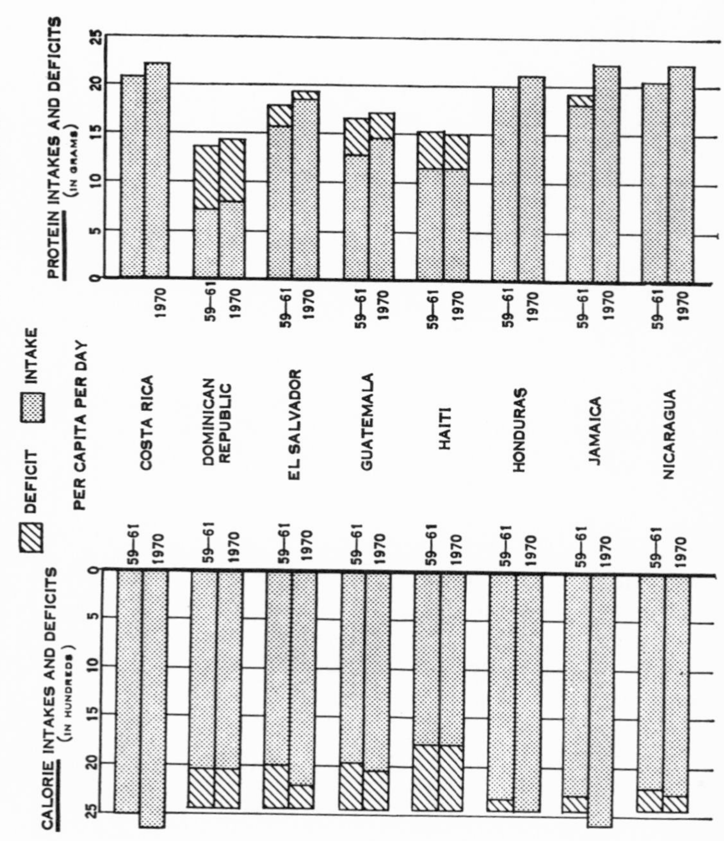
DEFICIT
INTAKE
PER CAPITA PER DAY
CALORIE INTAKES AND DEFICITS
(IN HUNDREDS)
PROTEIN INTAKES AND DEFICITS
(IN GRAMS)
0
5
10
15
20
25
COSTA RICA
DOMINICAN REPUBLIC
EL SALVADOR
GUATEMALA
HAITI
HONDURAS
JAMAICA
NICARAGUA
59—61
1970

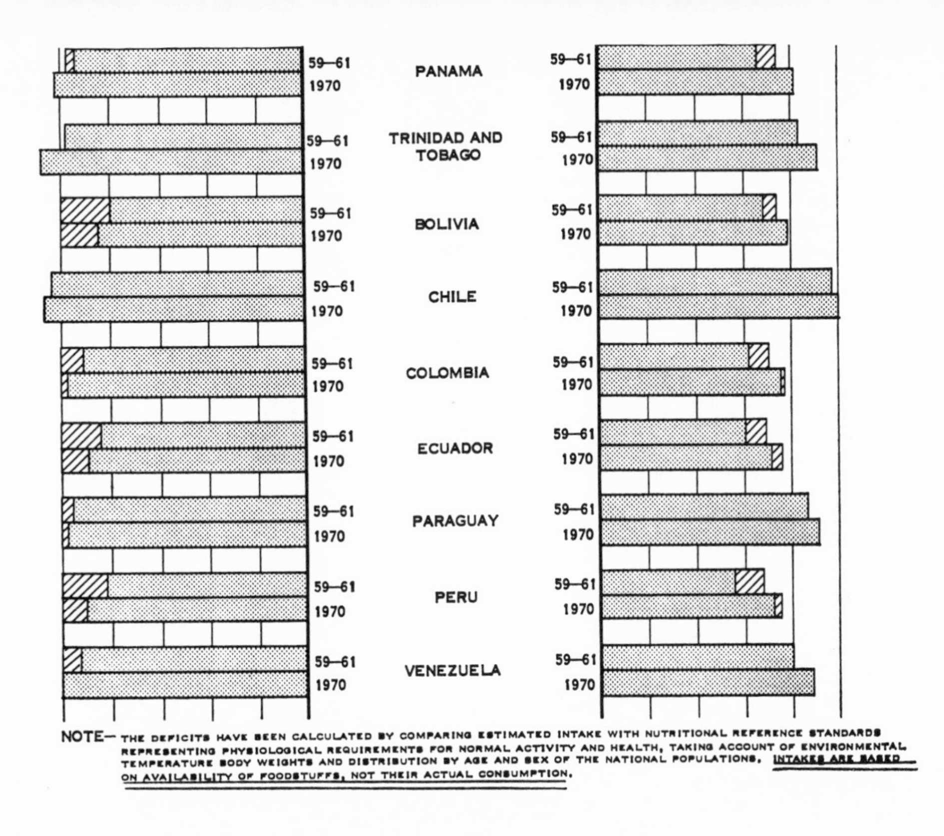
59—61
1970
PANAMA
TRINIDAD AND TOBAGO
BOLIVIA
CHILE
COLOMBIA
ECUADOR
PARAGUAY
PERU
VENEZUELA
NOTE— THE DEFICITS HAVE BEEN CALCULATED BY COMPARING ESTIMATED INTAKE WITH NUTRITIONAL REFERENCE STANDARDS REPRESENTING PHYSIOLOGICAL REQUIREMENTS FOR NORMAL ACTIVITY AND HEALTH, TAKING ACCOUNT OF ENVIRONMENTAL TEMPERATURE BODY WEIGHTS AND DISTRIBUTION BY AGE AND SEX OF THE NATIONAL POPULATIONS. INTAKES ARE BASED ON AVAILABILITY OF FOODSTUFFS, NOT THEIR ACTUAL CONSUMPTION.

double the present population—in less than thirty years.

This prospect—of more people than can be fed, employed, housed, or educated with present facilities—has brought a sense of urgency to the leaders of the twenty countries we visited.

In country after country, the problem of population growth, and the need for family planning to slow that growth, was voluntarily brought before the mission advisers—not only by physicians and public health officials, but also by educators, scientists, leaders of women's groups, economic ministers, and planning directors. Many stated plainly that they could not take a public position in favor of family planning because the issue of birth control in some hemisphere countries is too emotional and controversial. In private, however, they were candid and realistic.

"Our number one problem is population," a minister in Colombia told the mission.

A new impetus for family planning is coming from the women of Latin America, our mission advisers learned.

Enlightened by improved education, better informed than her forebears about what is going on in her country and her world, the Latin wife—especially if she lives in a city—is coming to believe that she has no obligation, religious or marital, to bring into the world a child she does not want and cannot afford to feed.

Throughout Central America, the Caribbean countries, and South America, leaders of women's organizations told the mission advisers of their efforts to promote interest in family planning and to broadcast knowledge about birth control. "And both the government and the Church turn their backs," one woman reported.

RECOMMENDATION: NATIONAL POLICY OBJECTIVE

The United States should recognize that the health problems of our sister republics are also our problems—for we share them, we are endangered by them, and we are moved to help deal with them.

RECOMMENDATIONS FOR ACTION

1. *The United States government should provide leadership in undertaking a special pre-natal and post-natal nutrition program, to be carried out throughout the Western Hemisphere by church, labor, women's, student, and other groups.*
   a. A concerted, hemisphere-wide program to mobilize all social forces, humanitarian instincts, and resources, including surplus U.S. food and available local products, could make the largest single contribution imaginable toward achieving the goal of a higher quality of life.
   b. This undertaking could draw on existing organizations such as the Catholic Relief Services, the Peace Corps, and the trade union movement, with added manpower from students mobilized in a way that will provide an opportunity to express in tangible form the idealism which motivates so many of the young in all countries. Its primary goal should be the proper nutrition of expectant mothers and infants, to halt the terrible effect on mental capacities now crippling a whole generation in many lands for lack of protein in pre-natal and post-natal diets.
2. *The United States should support the World Health Organization (WHO) and the Pan American Health Organization (PAHO) as the prime instruments of United States effort toward improving public health in the Western Hemisphere.*
   a. At present, the United States contributes 30 per cent of the World Health Organization budget and 66 per cent of the Pan American Health Organization budget.
   b. Agency for International Development (AID) loans and grants are concentrated on malaria eradication, community water supply, family planning, and nutrition.
   c. The Public Health Service (PHS) also is substantially involved in the inter-American health field, especially in the area of technical and professional training.
   d. As a general principle, multilateral programs as in WHO and PAHO are preferable to bilateral efforts

and give greater promise of achieving the staggering scale of effort which the size of the problem demands.

3. *The Technical Training Exchange Program set up by AID and the Pan American Health Organization with Public Health Service support should be broadened to provide greater opportunity for U.S. health professions personnel to study tropical medicine in Central American, South American, and Caribbean countries.*
   —Tropical medicine is sadly neglected in North America, but transportation advances bring not only progress but also the communicable diseases of distant lands. We have much to learn from South American doctors in this field.

J. Women

One of the most powerful forces for change and improvement in the quality of life in the hemisphere countries is the newly emancipated Latin woman.

Throughout the Western Hemisphere, women are becoming better educated, better informed, and less inclined to follow the tradition that women should be sheltered and subservient. Women's interests in the hemisphere nations cover all aspects of contemporary living, but they are increasingly active in their support of reforms in urban life, rural life, education, health, nutrition, environment, and politics.

To speed the process of change, women in the hemisphere are becoming political activists. They are eager to learn more about the techniques of political organization. And to a substantial degree they identify themselves with the forces of moderation—the middle-of-the-road.

Twenty years ago, women could vote in only five countries. Now they have the right to vote in every nation of the hemisphere, and they exercise that right. President Balaguer of the Dominican Republic openly credits his election in 1966 to women voters, who were enfranchised in 1965. He responded by appointing a woman as governor in every one of the Dominican Republic's twenty-seven provinces.

During the visits by the mission, leaders of women in every

country commented on the fact that this was the first time any President of the United States had ever sent his personal representatives to listen to the women of each country—and not just about women's activities, but about the full range of problems and opportunities facing each country.

In the discussions, the women leaders spoke with intelligence, sympathy, and candor. They cited irritants, e.g., the lack of interest in the United States in learning about other countries of the hemisphere, their disappointment in the Alliance for Progress, the U.S. strings on aid. But they spoke in a spirit of wanting to air and resolve their differences with the United States.

Their primary plea was for a much greater exchange—of people, ideas, educational methods, techniques for political organization, information about health services, social services, family planning, and day-care centers for working mothers. They want to exchange artists, writers, lecturers, scientists, and teachers. Through such exchanges, the women believe the hemisphere countries can develop closer ties and greater friendship with the United States, to the mutual benefit of all.

RECOMMENDATION: NATIONAL POLICY OBJECTIVE

The United States should recognize fully the expanding role of women in the political and economic, social and cultural development of the nations of the hemisphere.

RECOMMENDATION FOR ACTION

The United States, working through the proposed Western Hemisphere Institute for Education, Science and Culture, should increase its program of exchange in all fields relating to the role of women in developing the quality of life throughout the Western Hemisphere.

K. Communications

Fundamental to the accomplishment of the objectives and programs of the Western Hemisphere outlined in this report is better understanding among the people of the hemisphere.

This in turn rests on better communication between North and South America, and between the various nations themselves. This was a clear consensus of the 350 leading journalists and broadcasters in twenty countries with whom the mission had contact in its travels.

The Latin and Caribbean editors complained that the United States consistently gives them bad press coverage. Then they admitted that they are inclined to play up the negative aspects of the North American scene. They likewise print little news about their immediate neighbors.

It is also clear that the U.S. media have a limited and often uninformed interest in the news of Latin America and the Caribbean. North or south, the result is less than ideal communication among the peoples of the hemisphere.

Government leaders and news media officials in Central America and the Caribbean expressed considerable concern over Radio Havana's continued dominance of their air waves. In all but one Central American country, radio stations cut off at midnight and resume operation at 5 A.M. Radio Havana takes advantage of this with skillful communist propaganda aimed at the late-to-bedders and the early-rising farmers, most of whom have transistor radios. Radio Havana is even beaming programs in French and Creole into Haiti—one hour a day of each. The television, radio, and newspaper executives with whom we talked said that Radio Havana, with its powerful transmitter, does a more professional job than the Voice of America, which isn't widely heard because it is only on shortwave bands.

The Soviet Union spends over $1 billion a year on its foreign information programming, six times as much as the United States Information Agency. Communications is one of the three major channels through which foreign affairs are conducted—along with trade and diplomacy. The "transistor revolution" in the Western Hemisphere—bringing instant news of the world to the most remotely located peasant—makes it all the more crucial that a major effort be undertaken in the communications field.

RECOMMENDATION: NATIONAL POLICY OBJECTIVE

The United States by its own actions and in consultation and collaboration with its neighbors of the Western Hemisphere should do everything possible to improve communication among the peoples of hemisphere nations.

RECOMMENDATIONS FOR ACTION

1. *The over-all United States information program in the Western Hemisphere should be stepped up substantially.*
2. *A major effort should be made to make the Voice of America (VOA) at least competitive with Radio Havana in the Central American–Caribbean area, including improved programming and standard radio band broadcasting by VOA.*
3. *The President should invite a special team of United States experts on Western Hemisphere affairs to visit United States newspapers, magazines, and television stations, upon request, in order to improve United States media leaders' knowledge of the countries in the south.*
   —It is felt that discussions between the team of experts and media representatives would help increase the volume and accuracy of United States coverage of Western Hemisphere affairs. This would be particularly enlightening to telegraph editors, who make the daily qualitative judgments and decisions on whether to use or discard hemisphere copy on the newspaper wire services. The Inter-American Press Association could provide such a team; it is also suggested that a private foundation grant might be obtained for travel expenses.
4. *Greater efforts should be made to send United States journalists, teachers, intellectuals, writers, musicians, artists, and other representatives of the United States to other American republics.*
   —The United States State Department presently spends considerable money each year in bringing top journalists, artists, and others to the United States, but a better balance of this cultural traffic flow is needed. Hemisphere editors, for example, would welcome United States experts in the news media fields to con-

duct seminars in such areas as reporting in depth, improved newspaper makeup, and training of cub reporters. This could become a part of the program of the proposed Western Hemisphere Institute for Education, Science and Culture.

Chapter Five

CONCLUSION

This report has touched on a whole range of concerns that intrude upon the lives of Americans in the United States and throughout the hemisphere. The spectrum of these concerns is broad and the patterns are kaleidoscopic. Yet certain concepts emerge as fundamental:

People

The concern of man is man. And man must be the concern not only of his own government, but of all governments and all people. If we are not our brother's keeper, we are at least our brother's brother. If we fail in our awareness or commitment to this essential concept, we will have failed ourselves in a most critical way.

The Western Hemisphere as a Unity

Not only brotherhood but also geography and a common heritage of respect for the worth of man have united our hemisphere. No one can travel through this hemisphere without being keenly conscious of the multiple special links that bind it together. The Western Hemisphere nations are not separate entities; they are sovereign peoples indissolubly bound to one another by mutual hopes and needs, mutual interests, and common goals.

Every problem and opportunity before the hemisphere will yield to a better solution if it is not viewed in terms of "we" here in the United States and "they" in the other countries. The "we-they" approach is bankrupt and will defeat the aims of the policy-makers, and their people, who resort to it in the future.

The Western Hemisphere can achieve the common aspirations of its people only as a cohesive unit of free men.

THE CROSSROADS

There is a convergence of forces and events in the last of this century that is producing a crisis for free men:

—The scientific and technological explosion and the surge of industrialization it has produced;
—The consequent upward push in the standard of living for increasing tens of millions in the industrialized areas of the free world;
—The resulting increase in the gulf between the advantaged and the disadvantaged;
—The awareness both of the gulf and of the fact that it need not exist;
—A tidal wave of population;
—An uneasy nationalism, striving for self-identification;
—And a technology that tears at the fabric of all existing cultures.

However, we have within our reach the means—technical, political, and cultural—to shape these forces and to bring to all people in this hemisphere the fulfillment of their capacities and their own sense of worth.

Indeed, the fact that men believe this to be within their reach is one cause of the crisis of our times, since for all too many people in the United States and elsewhere in the hemisphere, indignity and degradation are their intolerable lot.

This crossroads—this challenge to our system of democracy and to the very survival of our values and ourselves—is not rhetorical. It is factual. Either we meet this challenge, or the prospect is for revolutionary changes leading we know not where. We have the values, the ability, and the means effectively to meet this crisis in the United States and in the hemisphere. We must employ these means with national dedication and determination, with subtlety and purpose. For the spiritual soil in the hemisphere is fertile for change—and the forces that would nourish revolution are ready and in place.

Interdependence of the Hemisphere

It is clear that the human resources and economic strength of each nation of the Western Hemisphere contribute to the strength of the others; that disease and propaganda cannot be trained to observe the limits of national boundaries; that the physical security of one enhances that of all; that a virus in the tropics will soon strike in the cities—and vice versa—whether that virus is biological or political; that violence in one nation uproots order and trust in its neighbor; that the bitterness and anger of one group erodes the good will of all; that confidence and courage and constructive concern in any one nation are contagious through the hemisphere.

The United States as Example

While specific problems differ from country to country, the fundamental thrust of the issues is the same throughout the Western Hemisphere. It is plain, accordingly, that we in the United States cannot effectively contribute to the forward growth of *our* nation and the hemisphere unless we manage the central problems of our time at home. Unless we are wholly to fail of our purpose as a nation, we must therefore meet the hopes of our own people for a decent and dignified life. Only if we do this can we lead, can we inspire, can we add to the quality of life for free men throughout the hemisphere.

A Course of Action

It is in this spirit that this report has recommended reorganization of the United States government's foreign policy structure, fundamental changes of U.S. trade and lending policies, renegotiation of foreign debts, and a more realistic division of labor in the hemisphere.

For the capacity of sovereign nations and free peoples to work together in mutual growth is crucial to survival—and crucial to the quality of life for those who do survive.

The achievement of such cooperation among the people of this hemisphere is the central objective of this report and of all its specific recommendations.

RECOMMENDATIONS FOR ACTION

That the President issue a major policy statement on the objectives of our Western Hemisphere relations and seek a joint resolution of the Congress to confirm those objectives so they become our recognized national policy.

—Such a declaration of policy by the Executive and Legislative branches would be a milestone in hemisphere affairs.

—It would have enormous impact throughout the hemisphere.

—It could be written as a first step in legislation to supersede the present encumbrances on Western Hemisphere policies and programs and to discourage similar new measures in the future.

—It should enunciate the principle that United States national interests must supersede those of any domestic special-interest group in the conduct of Western Hemisphere relations.

—It would convey a new character and style to our Western Hemisphere relations—one based on partnership, not dominance.

—It would help to create the framework for a new era of cooperation, progress, and human dignity in the hemisphere.

No man has ever lived and felt worthy of the gift of life who hasn't also felt tested by his own times. It is our good fortune to be tested in a time of accelerated change and extraordinary opportunity. It is our destiny to determine in our time that dignity for all men is achievable by a free democratic society in our nation, our hemisphere—and our world.